T0303752

SHANKS, YANKS
YANKS
AND
JÜRGEN

SHANKS, YANKS AND JÜRGEN

THE MEN BEHIND LIVERPOOL'S RISE AGAIN

BOB HOLMES

First published by Pitch Publishing, 2020

Pitch Publishing
A2 Yeoman Gate
Yeoman Way
Worthing
Sussex
BN13 3QZ
www.pitchpublishing.co.uk
info@pitchpublishing.co.uk

ISBN 978 1 78531 666 1

Typesetting and origination by Pitch Publishing

Printed and bound in Great Britain by TJ International Ltd

Contents

Acknowledgements

LIVERPOOL WERE conspicuous absentees from *Caesars, Saviours and Suckers*, my previous book on the good, bad and ugly among foreign owners of British football clubs. One reason was that the Reds' story still had some way to run and if Hicks and Gillett had been irredeemably bad and ugly, FSG were showing signs of coming good. If it was too early to judge them, with Jürgen Klopp on board, there was a real sense that a renaissance was under way.

Another reason? It's a book by itself. What encouraged me to go ahead was the manner in which Klopp was turning things around. As an unashamed Shankly groupie from way back, I began to spot similarities between 'the Normal One' and 'the One and Only'. Yep, any discussions of Liverpool FC managers will eventually lead to the Scot who became a Scouser.

Although 39 years since his passing, he's still omnipresent for those who grew up idolising his inimitable voice, outrageous quips and sheer force of personality. I just needed reassurance that I wasn't over-indulging in hero worship.

It came from Scousers, Dez Corkhill and Steve Darby, to whom I will forever be indebted for their generous support – not least in agreeing with the outlandish idea that Shanks was a factor in the Reds' resurgence! Steve's contacts were more than just obliging, with George Scott deserving a chapter of his own.

But the tales told by 'the 12th-best player in the world' are spread around several chapters and will soon be done even more justice in his own book, *The Lost Shankly Boy*. And thanks too to John Carrington of the website Red and White Kop for permission to reprint some of these tales. Mention also must be given to the great Kopite diaspora in Malaysia, where I live, for their support in this project.

Peter Hooton, the author of *The Boot Room Boys*, was kind enough to let me quote him directly from *Shankly: Nature's Fire*; Spirit of Shankly's Mike Nevin had a wise word on several issues, as did Paul Tomkins, Dom Matteo and *Anfield Wrap*'s Gareth Roberts. Shanks's only grandson, Chris Carline, was an absolute gem with tales about his beloved granddad, while Tony Murphy, Stephen Lawrence, Paul Moran and Nassos Siotropos all gave valuable insights. And David Kershaw recalled how Shanks helped mend a broken heart.

Award-winning football scribe and fellow Forest fan Daniel Taylor was kind enough to let me 'borrow' a Shankly story out of his own labour of love, *I Believe in Miracles*. The *Sunday Times*'s Jonathan Northcroft gave his views on Hicks and Gillett and lots of encouragement.

Elsewhere, I've indulged in a fair bit of 'fair usage' with bits and pieces from the *Liverpool Echo*, the *Anfield Wrap*, the This is Anfield website, *The Guardian*, *The Observer*, *The Independent*, *The Times* and the *Daily Telegraph*. Books quoted are Adam Powley's and Robert Gillan's *Shankly's Village*, Brian Reade's *Epic Swindle*, Stephen Kelly's *Bill Shankly*, Dave Bowler's *Shanks*, Raphael Honigstein's *Klopp: Bring on the Noise* and Dr James Walvin's *People's Game*. The BBC films, *The Football Men* and *Shankly: Nature's Fire*, were also a valuable source.

Foreword

by John Dykes

Asia-based broadcaster and journalist specialising in English football

I FIRST became aware of Bill Shankly as a kid growing up in 1970s Britain. My father would chuckle his approval of the legendary manager's pithy opinions and public pronouncements about building a winning mentality, taking pride in your community and understanding the privileges that came with representing Liverpool FC. Dad was a Newcastle-supporting Geordie who had relocated to the south and we were more disposed to watch Bobby Robson's Ipswich in action, but it was impossible to avoid Liverpool's dominance, or to do anything but admire English football's all-conquering force during and after Shankly's reign.

Fast forward a few years and journey with me from East Anglia to Southeast Asia where things haven't changed a whole heap. During my career here as a broadcaster, primarily of Premier League football, Liverpool have continued to dominate the agenda. My work has seen me rub shoulders with former Reds Steve McMahon, Robbie Fowler and Michael Owen, and our TV fan forums and talk shows are dominated by Liverpool chatter. Then there are expatriate Scousers like coach Steve Darby and commentator Dez Corkhill, with whom I regularly cross professional paths, and they're never short of a shared Shankly anecdote or epigram that they feel rings as true today as it did in the 1970s.

They're right. Jürgen Klopp may be conducting the Anfield choir these days but the tune he's getting out of both the fans and his team alike echoes with reminders of Shankly's ethos. Bob Holmes recognises this and expertly weaves the Great Man into his affectionate and insightful study of Liverpool Football Club's journey from those formative Cavern Club days to Klopp's Heavy Metal era. As Bob confided in me, he may have set out to write about ownership and its effects on the football club, but he soon realised that Liverpool's recent return to Euro-dominance has been in many ways built on the principles first laid down by Mr Shankly.

In these pages, Bob trains his probing journalistic eye on the various parties who have enjoyed temporary stewardship of the Anfield club down the years and sets out to assess their standing in the eyes of those who matter most: the fans of Liverpool Football Club. He masterfully juxtaposes Shankly's acerbic sayings with Klopp's rumbling bonhomie. Whether you are a newcomer to LFC or a seasoned observer who knows full well that football life started way before the Premier

League came into being, there's much to enjoy here. As Shankly himself once said, 'I was only in the game for the love of football – and I wanted to bring back happiness to the people of Liverpool.' There's much here to be happy about.

Preface

IT'S A bit of a stretch, but one that a man for whom exaggeration was an art form would surely have approved. Put simply, this book maintains that while much of the credit for Liverpool's return to their perch goes to their German manager, American owners and players from the four corners, Bill Shankly still had a hand in it.

These pages are a reminder of what he stood for and his 'voice' is heard throughout. It's argued that in finding a kindred spirit in Jürgen Klopp, Liverpool have reverted to the Shanks template in relating to both players and fans – or at least as much as being a 21st-century conglomerate allows.

It's through Shanks's rheumy eyes that we look at the game's evolution since he emerged from the coal mine to stamp an indelible mark on its history. Although there are aspects of today's game that we can be sure he would have found repugnant, they wouldn't have stopped him conducting the Kop on big European nights.

It's 39 years since he died, but founding fathers, inspirational leaders, commanders-in-chief, spiritual guiding lights – and he was all of those – are entitled to a slice of any belated dividend. And as a larger-than-life figure whose premature death felt more larcenous than most, a few posthumous achievements are bestowed upon him.

He has no greater legacy than the Boot Room, the cubby hole-cum-dynasty that went on to rule Europe. And besides a statue, gates, a hotel and union in his name, there are those who took a while to accept that he really had heard the final whistle, leading scribes among them.

Stephen Kelly begins his biography with the line, 'I swear I saw him recently … the last man out of Anfield … switching off the lights.' Hugh McIlvanney mischievously hinted that by having had his ashes scattered at Anfield, Shanks might still come to Liverpool's rescue by 'getting in the eye of a visiting forward about to shoot'. And just a dozen years ago, James Lawton maintained that 'Shanks becomes not less but more relevant to the football of today, his dictums shining like ancient wisdom …'

In a game unrecognisable from the one Shanks knew, the club is again benefitting from their glow. After losing its way for two decades, it has rediscovered its stride – the Liverpool Way. Anfield is back as an impregnable fortress after almost being abandoned, the current team 'goes through brick walls and comes out fighting', and the Kop still 'frighten the ball'.

Certainly, the massive part played by supporters can be traced back to Shankly. And although he died before the global Kopite diaspora emerged, it was because of his communion with ordinary fans that he was likened to an evangelist. Many believe it was his missionary zeal that inspired the fierce loyalty to the club still in evidence today.

But it wasn't just the fans – it was everything. When Shanks arrived, he found a club languishing in the old Second Division. It badly needed a revamp and by devoting every sinew to the cause he built what now might be called Liverpool 2.0. – a vibrant, all-conquering, irresistible force that dominated the English and European game for three decades in the second half of the 20th century.

And it was in the late 70s and 80s especially, under successors Bob Paisley and Joe Fagan, that the most convincing of all the claims about Shanks's supernatural powers can be made.

But these foundations were shaken by Heysel and Hillsborough, and both the game and the club changed out of all recognition. There were cowboy owners, a near-desertion of Anfield and the threat of administration. Rescue came with the current owners, the fans playing a pivotal role. The leading lights called themselves Spirit of Shankly, what else?

The question many still ask is: What would Shanks have made of it? A very different club to the one he took over – like the game itself and having to reconcile his socialist values formed a century ago in the poverty of a pit village with today's Instagram millionaires.

Shanks was no dinosaur – far from it; throughout both his playing and managerial careers he was a man ahead of his time. Nor was he shy about badgering the board for big sums to buy players. And what was the Boot Room if it wasn't for discussing improvements and getting an edge on opponents?

Opinions differ but many ex-players feel he would have adapted as he was nothing if not competitive. Which is why Fenway Sports Group (FSG), for all their early ignorance of Liverpool lore, might just have been tolerated.

This book dares to suggest that the modern club's return to greatness has been achieved at least in part by remembering many of its founding father's principles. Had *Time* magazine been staging its 100 Most Influential People awards in his day, Shanks should have been a shoo-in ... long before Mo Salah. Although he was no soaring orator, his words resonated with the man in the street. And still do.

With Liverpool FC, all roads lead to Shankly. He has become a beloved reference point to anyone seeking to understand how wealthy, capitalist owners and his socialist values co-exist in a vastly different game. As Lawton put it: 'He becomes not less but more relevant to the football of today.' Especially to Liverpool FC.

Chapter 1

'Some people believe football is a
matter of life and death. I am very
disappointed with that attitude.
I can assure you it is much, much
more important than that.'

Bill Shankly

LIV-ER-POOL. SAY it slowly, say it quickly, say it
in a Scouse accent – those three syllables evoke more
sound and fury than any city in the world. Pound for
in-yer-face pound. The chant belongs to another era but
whether it's the Kop or The Beatles, Mersey beats still
resonate with much of mankind. Football and music:
they are, above all else, what the place has been about
since the 60s.

Liverpool is a city of dynamic duos: Shankly and
Paisley, Lennon and McCartney. And stark contrasts:
grand buildings and Robbie Fowler houses; great ocean
liners and a 'Yellow Submarine'. It grew rich on the slave
trade yet is the birthplace of the man who abolished it.

Once the second city of the British Empire, for half a century it has been a hotbed of socialism. It's a city of 'A Hard Day's Night' and 'You'll Never Walk Alone' and, in the 60s, whether the sound was coming from The Cavern or the Kop, it was the most happening city in the world.

In football, those three syllables never meant more than when delivered with an Ayrshire rasp. There was something in the way Bill Shankly spat out his words, according to *The Guardian*, 'as if with a Gatling gun'. Long before it was claimed that Scottish was the most reassuring of British accents, Shanks had listeners in the palm of his hand. It wasn't that his voice was that deep or his accent that strong, but his tone, combined with a gaze that could penetrate the soul, got attention, respect and fear.

He wasn't religious but when it came to football he possessed an evangelic zeal. His tongue could be silver but had a serrated edge. And when he was silent, none spoke more eloquently for him than those he sent on to the field. Football is 'terribly simple', he used to say, and he got his players to let their feet do the talking. 'Pass and move' was his mantra and he called it 'the Liverpool Way'. For three decades the Reds dominated the club game and, although he didn't stay to reap his full share of the harvest, he had sown the seeds, created the template and built the foundations. Bob Paisley would win more silverware but Shankly was the founding father, the guiding light, the Merseyside messiah.

CHAPTER 1

The Red half will never forget its early European nights when the Kop cascaded like a human Niagara and the Liver Birds nearly took off in fright at the din. For years, the club has been desperate to return to the glory days but was striving – and frequently stumbling – in an unrecognisable game. No longer simple, it's now a global business complicated by three of Shankly's pet hates: high finance, agents and greed.

Shankly has been dead for 39 years but for those seeking to make sense of the current circus, his name crops up more than ever in both search engines and conversation. As many still mourn him, new converts embrace his principles, his beliefs, his way.

By 1991 – ten years after Shankly died – the Reds had taken their tally of league titles to 18, but they didn't add to it until 2020. In that time, they sometimes took their eye off the ball, strayed from the template and forgot his values. They have inscribed his words of wisdom on the training ground walls, but they also spawned the misplaced swagger of the Spice Boys. Shanks's dad was a tailor but white suits at Wembley? That was just one of the contrasts. Another was: kings of Europe in 2005, nearly bust in 2010.

Liverpool will be forever scarred by tragedy at Hillsborough and shame at Heysel, innocent victims at one, a few bad-apple perpetrators at the other. It can be a caring, Shankly socialist city but also one of attitude, cynicism and edge. It's a great city and a horrible city; the people can be the salt of the earth, the scum of the earth. Its finest hours can be spine-tingling, its worst moments heart-sinking. It's a people and port city, where millions have been welcomed and waved off, and where certain people have been told to fuck off.

Most of all, it's a spunky, don't-suffer-fools kind of place. All the more amazing then that a pair of 21st-century cowboys, six-shooter patter blazing, could swagger through the Shankly Gates as if they were the swing doors of a Wild West saloon. Even more incredible that they should get their trigger fingers on the crown jewels – Liverpool FC. That's what happened – give or take a freight train of bullshit and smarm – when Big Tom and the Wisconsin Kid conned their way into becoming the first foreign owners of the five-time European champions. And they did it by playing a £300m card trick on a panic-stricken sheriff.

They had spouted false optimism about 'a spade in the ground' and were carried shoulder high after a win over Barcelona. The bearers still have the scars. For the club and Shankly's legacy, Tom Hicks and George Gillett couldn't have been worse. Showing serial disdain for this fabled institution along with their true vulture-capitalist colours, they lied about their wealth and plunged Liverpool FC into debt. The 2008 financial crash came, and oblivion loomed. For Kopites it was the ultimate nightmare.

In their dreams, Shankly and Paisley wouldn't have allowed it to happen. Bob would have parked his tank that helped defeat Rommel outside while Bill would have growled, chewed them up and spat them out. The phrase 'turning in his grave' might have been invented for this scenario – even though Shanks was cremated. It was already more than a quarter of a century since his death, and everything he had built and all the values he stood for in life were under threat. To the Red half of Liverpool and its great global diaspora, there was nothing more important than that.

Rescue came from unlikely quarters: a Chelsea-supporting toff, another American venture capitalist and, ultimately, a manager from Germany. Martin Broughton, who was drafted in by a bank and was a season ticket holder at Stamford Bridge, played a blinder. FSG proved the acceptable face of capitalism and Jürgen Klopp ... well, many feel Shanks would have loved him.

Chapter 2

*'Even when I was in the pit, I
was only killing time ... I believe
I had a destiny.'*

Bill Shankly

HEWN, NOT born, is how many claim Shanks
made his debut in this world. A chip off Ailsa Craig,
that granite islet off the Ayrshire coast, maybe? A
more educated guess is that he was mined. Since the
Napoleonic wars, his home village of Glenbuck had
been a rich source of coal but, to borrow an immortal
line, 'in that rich earth, a richer dust concealed'. The
mother lode was footballers and he was the finest.

The pits have long since shut and the area is now
known as the Scottish Carboniferous Research Park.
The people have disappeared too, and Glenbuck is no
more than an eerily deserted shrine to its most celebrated
son. But to geologists it's as important as the Hadron
Collider is to particle physicists. What a name for a
marauding wing-half, he might have quipped.

'Young Wullie', as they called him, was never going to be anything else – before becoming a manager for the ages. With four older brothers all turning pro, 'fitba' was in his marrow and his *raison d'être*. His brothers would open up the pathways and the networks of the professional game. As he would write in his biography: 'I knew it would only be a matter of time before I became a professional player with one club or another. Even when I was in the pit, I was only killing time – I had to make a living – until the time came when I would be playing football. It was all worked out in my mind. I knew I had something to offer and I have always been an optimist. If I'd had to wait for a few years, it is possible I might have lost my enthusiasm. But I was young, and I felt somewhere along the line I was being guided. I believe I had a destiny.'

He went down the pit at 14 and although too young to work on the coal face, he had a sneak preview of its wretchedness. He breathed its lung-clogging air and peered into its unforgiving blackness. Although only 'killing time', he knew if he stayed too long, time would be killing him. Coal dust was always in his face, up his nose and in his mouth. It got in his eyes, too. But it couldn't stop him from seeing that a life down there would be a shortened life – and one of back-breaking toil.

He helped fill the coal trucks, which ponies pulled and boys like him shoved along the rails. He was paid half a crown a day. 'At the back of the pit,' he wrote, 'you realised what it was all about: the smell of damp, fungus all over the place, seams that had been worked out and had left big gaps, and the stench ... People got silicosis because they had no decent air to breathe. We were filthy most of the time, and never really clean. It was unbelievable how we survived. You could not clean all the parts of your body properly. Going home to wash in a tub was the biggest thing. The first time I was in a bath was when I was fifteen.'

The thought of stretching those contorted limbs on sweet-smelling grass, ball at their feet, breathing fresh air under a blue or, more often, grey sky was what sustained generations of young Ayrshire men. Passing and moving, laughing and joking, dreaming of escaping was what they lived for, Shankly more than most. Even underground he was stretching his limbs all the time, in perpetual motion along those rails. Years later, he would tell the *Cumberland Sports Weekly*: 'We [boys] felt so full of life coming out into the daylight after a hard day at the mine, those impromptu games that we had were fought out at a terrific pace. Knocks were numerous but no one bothered as we were as fit as fiddles.'

Fighting bulls have shown more reluctance to leave the corral than the teenage Shanks did to exit the hoist at the end of his shift. Charging home to lace up his boots, he would play till darkness fell. Games that began on Friday night were sometimes not finished till Monday morning. He would play all year round and his natural talent and insatiable drive earned him a place with the top local teams. They were the stepping stones to professional clubs further afield.

The village somehow managed to be both an outpost and a hotbed – but had none of the trappings of football enclaves today. Too remote for players to live in once they had joined a big club, it relied on portions of their wages being sent home, not to flaunt but to aid survival. Working-class people knew their place and even the biggest names in football were more like serfs than celebs. Grudgingly, they accepted their lot. As Gray's *Elegy* puts it, 'Chill penury repressed their noble rage.' Today's riches weren't even a twinkle. There was no such thing as bling, limos were only for the mine owners. Nor were there WAGs – just housewives who seldom strayed from the kitchen sink. The only 'groupies' were the rats that perched on the miners' laps as they ate their sandwiches, the only 'tattoos' the grime they couldn't scrape from their pores.

The few blurred images of Glenbuck that exist could pass for medieval etchings. In one, a couple of women glance furtively from their doors; the men, presumably, are underground. The only 'traffic' is a pony and trap. There were a few huddled cottages but most of the houses were terraced with small windows. The view was no picture postcard.

'Young Wullie' was one of ten children – five boys and five girls – who lived in two adjoining cottages where the dividing wall had been knocked down. There was no electricity or running water. The midden (toilet) was outside. The only heating was from the black stuff for which the men paid such a high price. Sharing was the only way they survived; they shared beds and baths, every morsel on their plates, every shred of clothing, every item they possessed. It was a geological age from *la dolce vita* of their 21st-century counterparts.

But they had something today's millionaires cannot buy – a community spirit. When players returned home, they didn't just sign autographs, they had kickabouts with the kids. Coping with the hardships, whether with family or friends, shoulder to shoulder, hand to helping hand, bred a toughness and togetherness that the 'Me First' generation cannot conceive. Greed wasn't good in those days – it wasn't an option. The wolf had yet to hit Wall Street – it hovered at every door.

The joys of life were basic, the basics elemental. There was no gated community for them to live in – the community left their doors unlocked anyway – and electricity was only for the mine. 'It was like Piccadilly Circus down there,' Shanks noted. It said it all that the happening hub of the village was underground. On the surface, there was only quiet desperation. Of the must-have adornments that today's prima donnas cannot live without, there were none.

The 20s may have been 'glorious' for some but those living on the East Ayrshire coalfield never got a mention in *The Great Gatsby*. Shanks compared it to 'Outer Mongolia' in its proximity to civilisation. Nope, there wasn't a lot there even by the hand-to-mouth standards of the day. Shanks's father, John, had been a top athlete – a quarter-miler – in his youth, and was a tailor by trade. In Glenbuck his living wouldn't come from making suits but from alterations. A disciplinarian, teetotaller and non-smoker, his sons were never going to become hippies. They also inherited his stamina and dress sense. In the 60s and 70s when sweaters and tracksuits were common attire for managers, Shanks would always be smartly turned out – even in the dugout.For all the hardships, 2 Monkey Row, Auchinstilloch Cottages was a happy household. The family would entertain themselves. 'We listened to the wireless or read the papers, so we knew about Jarrow [the protest march] and what was happening to other miners,' he remembered. 'But we were cut off from the big cities, so we talked to each other and about each other. We had fun, jokes, laughs and exaggeration.' The taller the tale the better for Shanks – 'exaggeration' would become an integral part of his team talks.

Although 'Dad' read the bible it wasn't an especially religious house; football was what the boys worshipped. Mum was a little less strict than Dad. Like all the Glenbuck women, Barbara Shankly fought a rearguard battle against coal dust, yet still managed to be house-proud. But she wouldn't do anything to discourage her boys from pursuing their escape route. As she cooked Sunday dinner, she allowed Bill and her next youngest son, Bob, to play head tennis with balloons over the table.

Treats would be solely at Christmas or on birthdays and be no more than an apple or an orange in a stocking. The highlight for young Bill was when his dad took him to the cinema in Muirkirk to watch American gangster movies. It was eight miles on foot there and back, and the films made a lasting impression. He loved the tough little guys, especially James Cagney, whose machine-gun manner of speaking he would come to imitate. As a manager, he would even show clips of shoot-outs to his players if they thought training was too hard. Gangster shoot-outs.

But take football away and the pit was the only career opportunity. And when the pits closed with the General Strike in 1926, there was only despair. 'Young Wullie' Shankly was 13 and in his last year at school. For him it might have been inscribed on his forehead in coal dust that football was the only way out.

Chapter 3

'Our football was a form of socialism – and the reason for our success.'

Bill Shankly speaking to Labour Prime Minister
Harold Wilson, who was a guest on his radio show

IN FOOTBALL'S formative years, there were no nation state owners, no multi-sport franchises nor clubs that were global brands – most were run by churches or factories, and the ancillaries were rudimentary. Long before it began to morph into a Disneyfied entertainment industry, the nearest thing football had to corporate hospitality was a cup of Bovril, the only 'assistance' for the ref – if he had upset the home fans – would be an early bath in a nearby pond. Half a century after the game had wrestled free from the mob, much about it was still mercifully medieval. But the way it was played in Scotland, the tactics might have come from Pep Guardiola's iPad.

North of the border, 'fitba' was a tough old gig, played on either quagmires or bone-hard pitches but always by bone-hard little men. Rich in talent, hard as nails, but often undernourished, they were dubbed 'hungry, hungry boys'. They came mainly from factories and mines, where they shared food – not enough of it – while on the field they shared the ball where the helpings were generous. 'Pass and move' was as much the credo of the times as the pressing game is today. It was about looking out for each other, finding a team-mate in space and then finding space for a team-mate to offload to you. 'The art of the game,' explained Hughie Knox, a leading Scottish coach in the early 1900s, 'is to make the ball do the running around.' Knox was a century ahead of his time.

The method arose partly due to the conditions – often windy, sometimes wet – while no one could survive the awkward bounces without a good first touch. And sometimes there was no bounce at all. If necessity was the mother of the passing game, Robbie Burns was its father. The Scottish Bard died long before football was organised, but his socialist-leaning works would permeate every aspect of life – including football. 'Burns was a living tradition in the mining communities of the early 20th century,' says football historian Bill Kay. Speaking in the BBC's Shankly documentary, *Shankly: Nature's Fire*, Kay adds: 'Miners were at the vanguard of the working-class movement, which had all sorts of activities, including Burns clubs and football clubs.' It's a view reinforced by Hugh McIlvanney in another BBC production, *The Football Men*. Noting that 'three of the greatest managers in British football were born in mining communities within 30 miles of one another', he tells viewers: 'Their understanding of teamwork and camaraderie was absolutely in the marrow.'

Shanks chose the *Life of Robert Burns* as his book on *Desert Island Discs* and embraced his work like a religion. He applied it to football and would become its messiah. 'Control and pass,' he would say. 'Pass and move, this is it. Get an early ball and so it goes from me to someone else: it switches it around. It was give-and-take – football socialism.' It was a line he would repeat to none other than Harold Wilson on his radio show after retiring. He told the Labour Prime Minister: 'Our football was a form of socialism – and the reason for our success.' McIlvanney added: 'The sense of being in it together was immensely powerful. There was a strength about it, a feeling there was never any doubt about their conviction, they were as good as anyone on the planet and they were prepared to let people know that.'

In its infancy in England, football was of a different political – and tactical – hue. Yet to be called the people's game, it didn't have quite such a hold on the masses – cricket and rugby were popular alternatives. The weather was a little kinder as were the pitches. But the biggest difference was the ethos. The early engine room of the game had been the public schools where posh boys were reared to run the Empire. On those manicured lawns, the individual was king – or at least a potential governor of a colonial outpost – and responsibility was encouraged. Passing to a team-mate was frowned upon, considered shirking and even cowardice!

So, the game that developed south of the border was basically a more selfish 'look-at-me' dribbling version. Fabled amateur club Corinthians deliberately missed penalties, which they deemed 'ungentlemanly'; if an opponent was sent off, they withdrew one of their own players to even things up. They were a quaint exception, but certain amateur traits inevitably spilled over into 'lower' schools and the working-class game. In his in-depth history of football, *The People's Game*, Dr James Walvin wrote: 'Where so many of Glenbuck's players scored over rivals was the spirit of teamwork which existed within the village. The air of mutual co-operation, which permeated every aspect of village life, meant that on the field, players would instinctively combine with one another, would share the responsibility of play and would not indulge in any selfish ball playing.' So, despite their numerical advantage in population, in the early internationals the English 'Ronaldos' were no match for the Scottish 'Xavis' and 'Iniestas'.

The playing fields of Eton may have helped win the Battle of Waterloo, but in football, a gung-ho spirit wasn't enough against a hard-nosed collective. The Scots won ten of their first 16 cross-border encounters. English clubs, especially in the north, took note and began to add the canny Jocks to their ranks. Such was the scale of the influx it changed the English game and led to it becoming professional. Now known as 'the Scots professors', the hungry boys had given plenty of food for thought.

CHAPTER 3

They also taught the English that football was a game for men not boys. Games between neighbouring Scottish villages weren't for the faint-hearted. The result mattered and they didn't take prisoners. The public school 2-0-8 line-up (two defenders and eight attackers) was as much a suicide note to the Scots pros back then as it would be for today's managers. Taking part might have been fine for the Olympics, but in the cut and thrust of football it was about winning. It was a lesson that stayed with Shanks for life.

Ironically, his first two clubs had a curiously 'posh' ring to their names. Glenbuck's very own team was called the Cherrypickers, while his next was also a bit of a mouthful – Cronberry Eglinton. But any opponent expecting a Corinthian approach from either would have had the rudest of awakenings. The Cherrypickers were named after the Glenbuck boys who, after joining the 11th Hussars under Wellington, had battled Napoleon's troops in a cherry orchard during the Peninsular War. Eglinton was the name of the local ironworks; tackling came straight from the smelter.

Another invaluable trait Shanks took from his upbringing was a never-say-die spirit. 'Never give up,' was a mantra he would instil in all his teams, 'not even when 3-0 down with five minutes to go.' In the greater game of life such communities as Glenbuck felt they were 3-0 down before they kicked off. But they battled on no matter how unlevel the playing field.

Their own field – Burnside Park – ceased to exist when the colliery finally shut down and the pumps stopped working – a tragic footnote to their interdependency. And after it became a lake, the Cherrypickers disbanded. Shanks had played only one game for them and such a devastating double blow might have derailed an 18-year-old less bullish about his destiny. The village went into terminal decline but the scion of the Shankly clan was too good a prospect to be forgotten. Cronberry snapped him up. But it solved only one of his problems; there was no other work and he signed on the dole.

Meagre though his wages had been, they would be missed. Only Shanks would have spent a chunk of them on the train fare to Glasgow to watch Rangers or Celtic. It's a tribute to the Shankly household that although staunchly Protestant, they had no truck with the sectarianism that was rife in the West of Scotland at the time. And despite being a Rangers fan, 'young Wullie' wasn't averse to watching the odd Celtic game if it meant seeing a decent match on a Saturday afternoon. It was heresy to many – but to him 'fitba' counted for more than religion. The absence of the bigotry that divided Glasgow and beyond was an attitude that would win him so many hearts in Liverpool, where there were also bipartisan feelings, although much more diluted.

Chapter 4

*'At our peaks, the five of us
could have beaten any five
brothers in the world.'*

Bill Shankly

GLENBUCK, A deprived village on life support from
a dying industry, had been an unlikely sporting El
Dorado. Brazil's *favelas* teem with footballers, South
Wales boasts a vaunted 'fly-half factory', while in the
north of England, a shout down a mine shaft once
summoned a fast bowler. Africa's Rift Valley is still
brocaded with long-distance runners. Yet nowhere can
compare with the East Ayrshire/Lanarkshire coalfield
– at either elite or workaday levels.

Within a sparsely populated 30-mile triangle, it
produced three of football's immortals – Shankly, Sir
Matt Busby and Jock Stein. If we include Bob Paisley,
Brian Clough and Sir Alex Ferguson in a managerial
'Mount Rushmore', the earlier trio would still be the
Washington, Jefferson and Lincoln of the British game.

As for players, Glenbuck alone nurtured no less than 50 professionals from a village of never more than 1,700 souls (and mostly a few hundred) in just three generations. Or, at its peak, one in every 35 inhabitants. It's enough to have Manchester City and Chelsea taking soil samples. Both have spent fortunes on their academies – City some £200m on their 238-acre training campus, while Chelsea leave their loan stars around the long-term car parks of Europe's second tiers. For all that, neither has produced a first-team regular.

The 'Glenbuck 50' established themselves at top-flight clubs both north and south of the border, including heavyweights such as Rangers, Celtic, Liverpool, Everton and Spurs. Six played for Scotland, four won the (English) FA Cup. Shanks did both. All five Shankly boys turned pro and, in what could be seen as the shape of boasts to come, Bill claimed: 'At our peaks, the five of us could have beaten any five brothers in the world.' So just what was concealed in that rich earth that produced so many players?

Tough areas breed tough people, but hardship alone cannot explain the number of graduates from what Scots football scribe Roddy Forsyth called 'the permanent night school of adversity'. Football was the perfect antidote to those darkened classrooms, the light at the end of their constraining tunnels. Every boy who could trap a bag of the black stuff would glimpse it and dream. After school and then after work, rain or shine, they would hone their skills for hour after combative hour. The pitch was across the road and the headmaster encouraged them to play. But it wasn't just about leisure; it offered a shot at liberation. Shanks would say: 'That was my apprenticeship in football, spent on coal-blackened fields near the pit-head.'

Once a tradition is established, the onus falls on succeeding generations to maintain it. In 1901, two Glenbuck boys, Sandy Tait and Sandy Brown, were in the Spurs team that won the FA Cup. As a token of gratitude, the Londoners allowed the famous trophy to be displayed in a Glenbuck village shop window. Here, the role models weren't remote figures glimpsed on a screen but real-life local boys who might even be relatives. In young Shanks's case, they couldn't be closer; his elder brothers were already beating the path to the professional game, while another guiding light was his dad, who had also played for the local team. After retiring from both track and field, John Shankly helped in the running of the club, dispensing advice on fitness and preparation. At his knee was his youngest son, a budding manager from the cradle. For all the other hardships and deprivations, in terms of the wealth of advice on his chosen career, paternal and fraternal, Shanks enjoyed a silver-spoon upbringing.

The Shanklys were one of three dominant families in the local football scene, and when the pros came home during the off-season – as Shanks would himself – they took the local youngsters under their wing. Impossible to imagine now, but such 'training sessions' amounted to simultaneous coaching, mentoring and inspiring. The teachers-cum-role models were trusted and idolised by the next generation. Modern technology apart, it's hard to see how such an 'academy' could be bettered. And in the wider scheme of things, it may begin to explain why, when it comes to youth development, an impoverished Scottish backwater puts today's nouveau riche super clubs to shame.

But if the modern academies ever sought to replicate these conditions, one key element would be missing. Indeed, it's a supreme and sobering irony that as today's football aristocracy lavish funds on youth projects, the secret of the greatest success story in producing home-grown talent was something money couldn't buy – it was the sword of Damocles dangling over the pithead.

Walvin argues that teamwork was far stronger in Glenbuck than anywhere else 'because of an almost permanent fear that the pits in the village would be closed'. And teamwork, he claimed, permeated every aspect of life. Fears about the impending loss of its only means of existence were passed down the generations. Glenbuck, more than any other village, suffered this ever-present danger. And over a prolonged period, besides increasing the levels of co-operation between villagers, it intensified the quest to make it into football. Escaping a life sentence on the coal face was one thing, the prospect of not even having it to fall back on was quite another.

In truth, though, there was nothing else to do. There was no other outside entertainment or diversion. Played every daylight moment and often in the dark, 'fitba' was truly the only thing. Girls played too, and the passion for the game was such that local trophy wins would be greeted with parades at which everyone turned out. Defeats hurt and weren't always taken gracefully – opponents were sometimes pelted with stones. One historian wrote: 'If you didn't know your football, you were out on a limb.'

Glenbuck may no longer exist but it's far from forgotten. The name is enough to attract pilgrimages from Liverpool fans happy to see a memorial stone in honour of its most famous son. It has also been featured in print and on screen. An academy has been set up in the surrounding area where kids are told of the deeds of ancestral neighbours. A peek at *Shankly: Nature's Fire* or the book *Shankly's Village* should have them lacing up their boots.

Fifty is an off-the-Richter number to emerge from such a small place, as co-author Robert Gillan points out. 'Per capita-wise,' he told CNN, 'it is the equivalent of a minor non-league club in London producing a quarter of a million players.' His fellow scribe Adam Powley added: 'There's something about the relationship between the workplace and sport that fused that identity in Glenbuck and enabled it to produce so many footballers. There's never been anywhere quite like it and it is unlikely there ever will be again. Liverpool's rise as one of the greatest and most storied clubs in the world was directly inspired by the ideals that Shankly grew up with and took from the village.'

Chapter 5

'I had no education so I had to use my brains.'

Bill Shankly

IT'S A pity Hollywood director, Stanley Kubrick, never turned his visionary gaze to the beautiful game. If he had, the movie maestro could have done worse than create a football epic along the lines of his *2001: A Space Odyssey*. For a dramatic dawn of this evolutionary tale, what could have been more compelling than the sight of a teenage Shanks, face blackened with coal dust, shoving trucks in a primeval underground scene? The cut could have been to someone like Pierre-Emerick Aubameyang driving his gold and diamond-studded Range Rover, supermodel by his side; or to a leopard skin-clad Neymar making a grand descent by helicopter to the roof of his Rio de Janeiro mansion, entourage in tow. Or any other of today's superstars who might match Imelda Marcos at the Boxing Day sales. Not as stunning as the jump from spinning bone to hurtling spaceship – acclaimed as one of the greatest cuts in cinema history – but another graphic illustration of unimaginable change. Only this one, about the fortunes of footballers, wouldn't have spanned four million years – just four generations.

Back when Shanks was still underground, the world economy was stalling, and the Great Depression loomed. With football still the working man's game, the wise money would have been on little green men landing from Mars before players became multimillionaires – before Alexis Sanchez picked up half a million quid a week for walking his dog; or before Ashley Cole 'nearly crashed' his car on hearing he was being offered only £55,000 a week; or before Pierre van Hooijdonk felt a £7,000 pay rise was only 'good enough for the homeless'. And the money would have been on little green men *winning* the FA Cup before a player blew £500,000 in a casino, and then gave a flunky £200 to buy a packet of fags, saying 'keep the change'.

Two hundred quid was a year's wages back then, half a million would have built a battleship. And it was before a dust-blown speck of a Gulf nation bought a Brazilian player for a club in Paris. That would have been hard to comprehend even before you could say £200m! Give or take a rocky outpost, that's what Britain raked in from its Empire in the 1920s. The big-spending player was, of course, Wayne Rooney, once hailed as a working-class hero.

To the pampered pros of today, Shanks's formative years may as well have belonged to the Middle Ages for all their relevance to the modern world. Yet after a limited education and an upbringing imbued with the values of the time, he built a sporting institution that's still among the finest, best-loved and most successful of its kind in the world. It has a history longer and more storied than some nations and boasts a following more passionate and devoted than some religions. Quite an achievement. As he put it: 'I had no education so I had to use my brains.'

First, though, he had used his brawn. One thing he could be grateful to the pit for was that it toughened him up. For all his innate strength, as a stripling of 18 and just 5ft 7in tall, he was a welterweight at best. And as a wing-half, he had to be ready for the heavyweight rigours of the professional game. He was more than prepared. The pit had been his gymnasium, the trucks his weights, the path along the rails his running track and the good class of local football his finishing school.

Shanks more than held his own against his hard-bitten elders and it wasn't long before the scouts came calling. When Carlisle United offered him a trial, he could have run there too, all through the Scottish Borders and English Lakes, he was fit enough. 'I ran 10 to 12 miles a day underground – marathon training,' he called it. So, he was off to new pastures – not rich ones but any old pasture was better than the dark, satanic seams of the pit. After impressing in a month-long trial, he signed to become a pro.

Although still raw, his natural talent and strength made him a prize catch for any league club. Carlisle were in the Third Division North, but he was on the ladder, and with his uncle, Bill Blyth, who had played for Rangers, a director at Brunton Park, the pathways and networks were already opening up. With dole queues wrapping themselves around Britain, his timing couldn't have been better. Economically, the country had never had it so bad. But Shanks, in the prime of life and on an eye-popping wage of £4 10s a week, had never had it so good. He wrote: 'I was much better off than a coal-miner for doing something in the fresh air that I would have done for nothing.'

Living in digs near the ground and close enough to home to happily pay the 12s train fare, Shanks soon adapted to his new life. After starting in the reserves as a bony 18-year-old in 1932, it wasn't long before he forced his way into a struggling first team. A model pro even as a teenager, he eschewed temptation, ate right and never took to smoking, drinking or, as he put it, 'gallivanting with women'. Following the strict tenets of the leading manager of his day, Arsenal's Herbert Chapman, he aimed to be at his physical peak for every game. Constantly thinking of ways to better himself and the team, he soon earned the respect of team-mates and admiration of fans for his wholehearted approach. Young Shankly was a rare ray of hope in a poor campaign that saw Carlisle end up a lowly 19th in the table.

His self-improvement extended beyond merely keeping fit through the close season. He worked on several aspects of his game, among them practising long throws over houses and he rounded up small boys to fetch the balls for him. He also coached older lads. Still to fully develop as a man or as a player, he was already a manager in the making. Brother Bob certainly thought so and quipped that Shanks's lengthy sessions with the kids were 'Bill Shankly's Soccer Sunday School'. Coaching kids and valuing the throw-in were just two things he would share with a certain Jürgen Klopp.

Just 16 games in that first season were enough for him to attract a wider audience. Showing his 'unlimited energy and uncommonly good ideas', as one critic put it, he became a target for bigger clubs. And Carlisle's hard-up board were eager to cash in. Preston North End, who had watched Shanks at Cronberry and had been a home from home for Scottish players for decades, made them an offer they couldn't refuse – £500. Life would get even rosier for him now that he was in a higher division with his earnings almost doubled.

Preston had a proud history, but they were now in the Second Division and the town was run down. Still, it didn't take Shanks long to make an impression and start talking up his 'great wee team'. It was 'wee', alright – half of them were Scots and just 5ft 6in or 5ft 7in tall. The great Tom Finney, a local boy yet to break into the first team, noted: 'We were taught the Scottish game – short passes – and keeping it on the deck.' They let the ball do the running around.

Although still developing as a player, Shanks was already ahead of his time. He began experimenting with hot and cold baths, different pre-match meals and five-a-sides in training. It was six decades before

Arsène Wenger changed the game and Shanks was still a rookie. A pen picture described him as 'the baby of the team who takes dynamite in his milk'.

His explosive presence in the middle of the park helped carry North End to promotion in his first season and the fans loved him. And when the young Finney finally emerged, it was Shanks who became his minder. Finney would later compare him with Bryan Robson 'in terms of his influence on the pitch and the way he would get others to play'. Liverpool fans might prefer it to have been Steven Gerrard, but to be compared to either, Shanks had to be some player.

Decades later, when Thames Television asked him what sort of player he had been, he stuck to his script: 'I was a socialist football player. I did everything. I gave 100 per cent. I was different, I was single-minded. I thought getting married would finish me – I knew I wouldn't be as strong as Samson if I got married! On a Sunday, I would go to the ground for a massage to start to get ready for Saturday's game even though the previous game had only just finished. I wanted to die a healthy man – when playing I wanted to be fit for every eventuality. If you are caught unawares, you are rubbish.'

That first season in the top flight Preston finished comfortably mid-table and reached the quarter-finals of the FA Cup – a satisfactory start to what would become one of the club's finest eras. Shanks was now a mainstay in the side and match reports often waxed lyrical about his 'tactical vision, positional sense' or just his 'leadership'. Another noticeable trait was how he shrugged off injuries. He thought most injuries were in the mind and it was a view he would hold as a manager as many a Liverpool player would discover.

His finest year as a player was 1938. After the bitter disappointment of losing the FA Cup Final of 1937 with seven Scots in the team, Preston made no mistake when they reached the next one, winning 1-0 over Huddersfield. Shanks had won his first Scotland cap against England at Wembley weeks earlier. He was only 25 and had most of his career ahead of him – or so he thought.

Preston couldn't follow that season, finishing in mid-table and losing in the quarter-finals of the FA Cup in 1939. But by now the drums of war were beating across Europe and neither life nor football would ever be the same. Just 26 when war broke out, he was robbed of six years of his prime. He joined the RAF the day after Winston Churchill's 'fight them on the beaches' speech but was never posted abroad and saw no action. For such an inspirational leader of men, it seems a wasted opportunity – there were those who felt he could have shortened the war! But his fire and brimstone qualities were submerged by mundane routine. Instead of punching holes in German lines, he was punching rivets into aircraft parts with only football to relieve the boredom. It was like confining General Patton to the canteen.

Football carried on – in a fashion. There were regional leagues and under the lax laws of unofficial games, Shanks, like many other top players, became a wandering minstrel who appeared for the club nearest to his posting. He still gave undying commitment, and Norwich, Cardiff, Arsenal and Partick Thistle were the beneficiaries. He achieved the rare distinction of winning wartime cups both north and south of the border and also turned out in several home 'internationals'. In 1944, he made his best ever 'signing' and married Agnes 'Nessie' Fisher, whom he met while she was serving in the WRAF in Glasgow.

Throughout the war he had kept fit, but by the time hostilities ended he was 32 and feeling a little less like Samson. He was made captain, but the new Preston star was Finney, who Shanks swore was the greatest player he had ever seen. Admiration was mutual, with Finney extolling Shanks's virtues as a leader. 'He might have been a seasoned professional,' said the Englishman, 'but would always come and talk to us at the end of each game and tell us how we could improve.'

But Preston weren't what they were and nor was Shanks. His discipline and fitness camouflaged it well, but he was no longer the irresistible force of pre-war. But it was still a cruel and premature decision to release him in 1949. He was also denied a benefit. Shanks raged in protest, but to no avail; back then directors still called the tune. After his final game, as he walked out of the club, he presented his No.4 shirt to manager Billy Scott and told him: 'It will run around by itself.'

He opted not to play for another club and, thinking that he might have to begin his post-playing career as a trainer, took courses in physiotherapy and massage. A wise precaution, quipped some, as he had been known to rub people up the wrong way. But he didn't have to wait long for an opening. It was old flame Carlisle who offered him his first chance to be the gaffer and he jumped at it. He felt he had absorbed all the coaching knowledge he needed and possessed the two key requirements of a manager anyway: 'I could speak common sense about the game and I could spot a player,' he wrote in his autobiography. The only surprise is that there's no record of him saying: 'I was born a manager.'

Chapter 6

'At corners, the Kop would frighten the ball.'

Bill Shankly

THE EARLY life of Bill Shankly was full of paradoxes. As we've seen, in spite of an unhealthy workplace he was extremely fit; in spite of rudimentary schooling, he had expert tutors; and although his upbringing was tough, he felt privileged – no one has ever had more career guidance from the cradle. And besides his immediate family, there was an uncle to help at this first club – and he was still there when he went back as manager. Yet for all that, his apprenticeship in the dugout, like his childhood, was served in bleak, impoverished backwaters.

But then he was in good company. Alex Ferguson had only eight players and no goalkeeper at East Stirlingshire, Brian Clough had to paint the stands at Hartlepool, while Jock Stein needed 'a magic wand' at 'doomed' Dunfermline.

And none of those had an uncle on the board.

For all his lofty ambition, Shanks was a pragmatist and knew that, for a Scot with strong family ties, Carlisle was a convenient stepping stone into English football. After all, he had gone there as a player and it was the nearest club for trips home, which pleased his wife. It hadn't changed much from when he was there the first time – still a one-horse town. It was the antithesis, then, of his ultimate goal of bossing a big-city club with a passionate crowd and a raucous atmosphere. But Carlisle would do for now.

Another of his virtues was a willingness to seek advice. Despite his natural exuberance, he was a good listener and, for all his experience as a player, accepted that as a gaffer he was driving with 'L' plates. But he never did anything by halves and didn't just pick the brains of senior players, he ransacked them. Every morsel could be of value, he felt, and his motivational powers and attention to detail soon took effect. Carlisle rose from 15th, when he joined for the last few matches, to ninth and then to third the following season.

He and Nessie now had a baby girl and lived in a terrace house near the ground to which he walked as he didn't own a car. It was the time of post-war rationing and, in the terrible winter of 1947, life was especially hard. To make sure they had a fire to keep the baby warm, Shanks would often scavenge a few bits of firewood from the neighbourhood. The irony wasn't lost on him that coal, too, was hard to come by – it was rationed.

So, much to his frustration, was cash for new players – or so it seemed. After a famous cup run in which Carlisle held Arsenal to a draw at Highbury before losing the replay, Shanks asked for funds to strengthen the team. Not unexpectedly, his request was denied. He hadn't failed to notice, however, that a job at a big-city club with a passionate crowd had become available. With nothing to lose, he applied for the Liverpool post and was surprised to be granted an interview.

Having played in England-Scotland matches at Wembley and Hampden, FA Cup finals and top-of-the-table clashes before packed houses, he lived for the big occasions, for the tingle in the spine. And he knew there was one set of fans who could raise the hairs on the back of his neck higher than anywhere else – Liverpool fans' fervour, he sensed, matched his own. 'At corners,' he remembered, 'the Kop would frighten the ball.'

The Reds were champions in 1947 but hadn't kicked on. As a visiting player at Anfield, he had always sensed a crowd craving for more. He felt the club was a sleeping giant held back by the board's lack of ambition. Although still cutting his managerial teeth, he made a big impression in the interview. The Liverpool suits were taken aback by his ideas and chutzpah, but not quite enough to surrender the privilege of picking the team. The one director who did vote for him was Tom Williams and it was he who would keep in view the file on this up-and-coming manager.

Undaunted, Shanks was determined to move on and, when Carlisle refused to stump up for new additions or promised bonuses, he jumped ship to Grimsby Town. In this fishing port there was no escaping the smell of its main industry. The football club was rudderless and demoralised, having just been relegated to the old Third Division North, but Shanks was soon telling the players they were 'pound for pound, the best in the country'. Those tall tales in the family home in Glenbuck were proving useful prep for the morale-booster role he now relished. And he soon had the Mariners playing as if they had caught Jaws in their nets. He introduced five-a-side matches in training and another of his hallmarks was demanding money for new players. There wasn't any and, with Nessie homesick and the east coast bleak even in summer, Shanks moved after a couple of seasons – this time to Workington. He did pick the glamour jobs.

It was a lot closer to Scotland but not as convenient as Carlisle. It was also, much to Shanks's chagrin, more of a rugby town – both league and union having a bigger following than football. And he had a rude awakening in just how far it was from … well, civilisation. When he searched for a light switch, he was told there was no electricity – the club was still using gas. The ground felt like the North Pole and the only place to avoid frostbite was the boiler room. It was there, huddled over a brew of tea amid paint pots, tools and other paraphernalia, where he would chew things over with the groundsman and the idea for the fabled Anfield Boot Room was conceived.

It was his third club and he would spend every waking minute racking his brains for ways to improve the team. No shingle on the beach was left unturned, no sliver of info ignored, no train journey wasted. When Workington were drawn away to Leyton Orient in the FA Cup, they had to go to Carlisle to catch the *Flying Scotsman* to London. On boarding the train, he heard that the great Hungary side were in another carriage. They had just beaten Scotland 4-2 at Hampden Park and were returning to the capital. The year before, they had famously thrashed England 6-3 at Wembley. Shanks immediately stalked the carriages in search of the legendary visitors.

He found them in first class. Undeterred by the language barrier, he got Ferenc Puskás's autograph and then went back to fetch his players. Known as the 'Magical Magyars', none of the Hungarians spoke a word of English so 'conversation' was minimal. But Shanks was jubilant and when Workington pulled off a surprise win the next day, he said: 'Some of their magic rubbed off on us.'

Another stunt was to try to persuade the great Stan Mortensen to join Workington – akin to asking Harry Kane to join Rochdale today. It would have been the transfer coup of all time but Morty went to Hull instead. A rare failure but it showed Shanks's ambition – he was irrepressible and clearly destined for bigger things. Sure enough, he soon took a step up by going to Huddersfield as assistant to old pal Andy Beattie. It wouldn't be long before Beattie quit, and Shanks was in the hot seat at another storied but seen-better-days small-town outfit.

Encouraged by having two budding world-class stars in Denis Law and Ray Wilson under his wing, Shanks went into overdrive. 'He made us feel as if we were the best in the world,' remembers Law. But another trait that would become infamous at Liverpool had the opposite effect – he had no time for injuries. If a player didn't have both legs in plaster, he wouldn't just get the cold shoulder, he would be sent to Shanks's version of the Gulag. *Persona non grata* didn't do it – he would be blanked, dropped and, in Shanks's mind at least, cease to exist. Forget back injuries and groin strains, if both legs had been amputated, Shanks would want to see the stumps – or so it was claimed. He lived up to the hard-man image, alright. He was, of course, always fit, didn't drink or smoke, took a full part in training and never fell ill, so he had no sympathy for those that did.

He was always on the lookout for good players and wanted to sign two emerging Scots, Ron Yeats and Ian St John, for the Terriers. But the chairman told him he couldn't afford to buy even one of them. It was a recurring theme, but he always seemed to think every director was made of money even if he were the local chimney sweep. John Henry may feel he dodged a bullet.

At Leeds Road, Shanks knew when he was appointed that there was precious little cash. No one called it 'Moneyball' then, but the club policy was to develop youngsters and, in Law and Wilson, he had two jewels. Law arrived as a squinty-eyed 15-year-old who was already attracting bids. Busby offered £10,000 for him but Shanks told the board: 'He'll be worth £100,000 one day.'

Law would become 'the king' at Manchester United and Wilson would win the World Cup with England (while at Everton). Both were sold after Shanks left but not before they helped him to a 5-0 win over Liverpool, whose directors, he remembered, filed out as if at a funeral. But for him it was the opening he had been looking for – he was about to get the chance to change football history.

Liverpool, relegated in 1954, were at their lowest ebb. They had been knocked out of the FA Cup by Worcester City – still the club's historic low on the field. The year before it had been Southend that did the damage. After successive humiliations of that magnitude, even a board that insisted on picking the team knew something had to give.

They had come perilously close to being like the pools 'winner' who forgot to post his coupon, but Tom Williams, who had since become chairman, now had enough support to ensure there was no repeat. But when he asked Shankly, 'How would you like to manage the best club in the country?' it was the Scot who made the faux pas. Shanks asked, 'Why? Is Matt Busby packing it in?'

Manchester United were a division higher back then and, nearly two years after the Munich tragedy, well into a rebuild. Liverpool had to do the same from a division lower. That answer was the last big mistake Shanks would make until he retired, but Liverpool weren't deterred. Neither they, Stanley Kubrick nor Nostradamus could have foreseen the future their new manager would build.

Chapter 7

'The socialism I believe in is
everyone working for each other,
everyone having a share of the
rewards. It's the way I see football,
the way I see life.'

Bill Shankly

THESE WORDS are inscribed on the walls of the
Melwood training ground, the Shankly Hotel and adorn
the Spirit of Shankly (SOS) website. They're etched
on the minds of millions of followers and plastered
everywhere you read eulogies to the great man. Neither
Marxist nor Maoist, they are but a simple expression of
the working-class values and aspirations of the time.

Shanks was born two years after the *Titanic* sank
and a year before the Great War began. Humble though
his origins were, his disciples can justly claim that
significant events happen in threes.

If the names of sporting and cultural icons carry
more resonance than their political or academic peers,

it's no stretch to call him one of the most influential British public figures of the late 20th century. Being one of the greatest football managers of all time was always going to earn him a place among the probables. But it was his wit, wisdom and sheer indefatigability that transcended the traditional boundaries. In short, it was the irresistible force of his personality that ensured a more enduring impact than the other two members of the immortal trio born in that fecund corner of the West of Scotland. He was larger than life.

Like Shankly, Stein and Busby did an awful lot more for their respective clubs and adopted cities than pick winning teams. Both were magnificent football men and admirably modest in life, but neither were blessed with Shanks's charisma or genius for the outrageous gesture or hilarious quip. Eulogised by Hugh McIlvanney in *The Football Men*, all were true maestros of their trade. Players weren't only willing to go through brick walls for them, they would replace the bricks and re-lay the mortar. And trust them with their lives. It was their incorruptible amalgam of sound judgment, fairness and football sagacity that made them father figures to players of different generations. In Shanks's case, he became a father figure to the people of Liverpool too.

No football club owes as much to one man as Liverpool FC does to Shankly. Not Manchester United to Busby or Fergie, not Celtic to Stein, not Arsenal to Herbert Chapman or Arsène Wenger, not Forest to Cloughie. And certainly not an entire city. With a successful team, a manager can lift the morale of a club's constituents, but Shanks's appeal crossed the normal demarcation lines. Even Evertonians, although taunted unmercifully by him for years, eventually came to acknowledge his contribution beyond the touchline. He had a gift for the sound bite that a politician would die for, and if it sometimes smacked of the fourth form, he could turn it into philosophy. Like Muhammad Ali, he made us cackle and question in equal measures. And if Shanks lacked the global audience that Ali had, to players, fans and especially Red Liverpudlians, he was just as inspirational.

Formed in 1892 – from Everton's rib if you want a Biblical parallel – Liverpool FC had won the league five times before Shankly arrived. But the Liverpool we know today didn't really take off until the 1960s. That was when Shanks, who called the club 'a shambles' on taking over in December 1959, began to work his magic. He didn't just stir a sleeping giant, he stoked the magma of a dormant volcano. And such was the eruption of spirit, pride and passion he wrought it was like a New Liverpool. And in the voice of the Kop, it became LIV-ER-POOL – those three syllables taking on a whole new significance.

But, as with Fergie at United, it didn't happen overnight. Shanks was shocked by the enormity of the task and hamstrung by the board's pallid indifference. It got so bad he was only talked out of quitting by, of all people, United's Busby. It will forever be the biggest favour that club has done for their arch-rivals.

So frustrated was Shanks by the situation that he forgot his maxim about not giving up. Busby, who had played more than 100 games for Liverpool as a wing-half, reminded him that he wasn't 3-0 down with five minutes to go, but the score was 0-0 and he had only just kicked off. Shanks listened to his fellow Scot, who was four years older and whom he respected, and decided to battle on. He gradually won the directors over, one by one. Eventually he would bring about a transformation the like of which has never been seen in one city before or since. Naples had a frenzied couple of years with Diego Maradona, but it didn't last; Shanks created a dynasty that has. Allied to a simultaneous awakening of the music scene, it turned Liverpool into the most culturally vibrant place on earth.

Back in 1959, the club didn't belong among the elite of English football; they weren't even number one in Liverpool – Everton claimed the bragging rights. Back then the Reds, who had done nothing for a dozen years, didn't possess the aura of Busby's Babes or Stan Cullis's Wolves. Those two were the teams of the 50s. Liverpool had the fans but were something of a one-man team. They were often known as Liddell-pool after the legendary Billy Liddell, their standout player and one of the greats of the post-war era. But even with him they were also-rans in the old Second Division.

Yet it was as if their fans had been waiting for Shankly's coming. Or at least a manager of his ilk, a leader whose ambition matched their own and whose every utterance inspired. Hailing from the game's richest spawning ground and an international player, it seemed his destiny to find its most atmospheric stage and appreciative audience. No one knew it at the time, but this wasn't merely 'the right fit' but a marriage made on the Elysian Fields.

If he hadn't ended up at Liverpool, you feel such a force of football nature would surely have made its presence felt elsewhere. But even with hindsight, it's hard to see it happening on the same epic scale. Nowhere else had the same burgeoning sense of localism or raging thirst for football fulfilment. Glasgow? The Scottish League wasn't a big enough stage and the city was riven by sectarianism. Newcastle? Shanks's disciple Kevin Keegan briefly hinted at something similar but couldn't sustain it. And long before anyone mentioned 'the Geordie nation' in the North East, Liverpool had forged its own distinct identity. More accustomed to immigrants than anywhere else – it had had a huge Celtic influx, mostly from Ireland but also Scotland and Wales – the city had shed its Anglo-Saxon reserve a hundred years ago. With people from the four corners, the cosmopolitan make-up bred a fiercely independent streak. By tapping into this as well as talking up the team, Shankly was able to harness the football hunger and 'Liverpoolness' to maximum effect. As Roy Evans would say: 'Shanks was very keen on making Liverpool FC a very fierce source of civic pride. His intensity never took a day off.'

But there was an awful lot of work to do to turn the team around. When he pointed his little Austin

A40 over the Pennines that December day in 1959, Huddersfield, the club he was leaving, were four places higher in the table than Liverpool. And his new club was in a bigger mess than he realised. Anfield had no means of watering the pitch, the toilets didn't flush, and the training ground looked, he said, 'as if the Germans had been over'. Jürgen Klopp would have enjoyed that. A decade and a half since the last Luftwaffe raid, and such talk still resonated. The idea of a German coming over to sit in Shankly's seat, wear his shoes and mould his team was an odyssey not on anyone's drawing board.

In 1959, Melwood was still used for cricket. The pavilion looked as if W.G. Grace might walk out to bat, while the outfield had more rough than Carnoustie. Then there was the team – also a bit wooden and in need of major repair. But it was on that first unpromising winter's day that Shanks made the best football decision of his life – to retain the team of coaching assistants, Bob Paisley, Joe Fagan and Reuben Bennett. He would sweep clean in other areas, but for the revolution he was planning, he needed trusty lieutenants. He even found a venue for them to brainstorm. Not much bigger than Workington's boiler room, the 12-ft-square cubby hole near the dressing rooms became the inner sanctum for football's most storied conclaves – the Boot Room was born.

Like any new broom, Shanks desperately wanted to hit the ground at a speed his Austin A40 couldn't reach. But his start was hardly auspicious: he lost his first two games with a combined 0-7 aggregate and his first signing was a dud. Crowds were below 30,000 and Nessie remembers he claimed his proudest early achievement was getting those toilets to flush. She also recalled that when Liverpool lost, he would clean the cooker to take his mind off it. Neither a cook nor a handyman, this was the most practical thing he did in the house.

Players he wanted – among them Brian Clough and Jack Charlton – were denied him, but as advised by Busby, he stuck at it. He introduced 'sweat boxes' in training where players had to react to the ball rebounding off wooden boards at different angles. It made them 'control and pass' not unlike Guardiola's famous *rondos*. Shanks would say: 'Liverpool's training is based on exhaustion and recovery, twisting and turning: a fit team has a tremendous advantage.' With Paisley holding a stopwatch, Fagan barking instructions and Shanks casting an all-seeing eye, it may have flouted the Geneva Convention, but the players daren't complain; they were all in it together.

Gradually, by sheer force of personality and changes to just about everything, his methods took effect. He drove the team to third place, although only the top two went up. But there was a new mood, as well as a new pitch at Melwood and crowds started to return. George Scott, who had joined as a 15-year-old from Aberdeen, remembers: 'Shankly brought fantastic self-belief, passion and enthusiasm to Liverpool Football Club and he demanded no less from us players. He used to say to us young players: "Without enthusiasm you are nothing." He also had tremendous character and a great sense of humour, and also loyalty. When he came to Anfield he kept all the backroom staff and forged a dynasty. He loved the supporters and they loved him. There has in my view never been another manager to compare to him in this respect.'

Shanks's first significant signing was Gordon Milne, for a bargain £16,000 from Preston, yet a Liverpool record. He was on his way – he just needed a stroke of luck. It came the following season from, of all places, Everton. Sir John Moores was Littlewoods Pools boss and a shareholder of both Everton and Liverpool. He also owned the Littlewoods chain of department stores so was anxious to keep the whole city – not just the Blue half – happy. He installed business partner Eric Sawyer as a director of Liverpool to help get them to join the Blues in the top flight. And in Sawyer, an accountant, Shanks found the extra ally that he needed. After finishing third again and with frustration mounting, he was even more determined to sign Yeats and St John. And in the summer of 1961, with Sawyer's backing, he finally got them. It was, as he would later acknowledge, the turning point.

The Milne fee was blown out of the water as they spent £22,000 on Yeats from Dundee United, and £37,500 on St John from Motherwell. Yeats, a towering centre-half and St John, a Jack-in-the-box striker, were instant successes. Liverpool were unstoppable, and in Shanks's third season (1961/62) stormed to the Second Division title. Local boy Roger Hunt scored 41 goals. Ian Callaghan had played the first of his 857 games for the club and Gerry Byrne was also emerging. Coming through the ranks were Tommy Lawrence in goal and tough boy-man Tommy Smith, whom Shanks described as '18 years old when he was born'.

So chuffed was he to get Yeats that he invited the press to meet him by saying: 'He's seven feet tall – you can come in and take a walk around him.' At 6ft 2in, Yeats was two inches shorter than Virgil van Dijk but a similar colossus in defence. Just like Klopp almost six decades later, Shanks was building the spine of the team, deciding on the men he wanted and waiting patiently – even a whole season – for them to come. Even though Klopp paid world-record fees for Van Dijk and Alisson Becker, his dogged pursuit of them has evoked comparisons with how Shanks did it.

Chapter 8

'It's like asking mice if they cared too much about cheese.'

Derek Hatton, when asked if Liverpool
people cared too much about football

IF IT was 'cometh the hour, cometh the man' for the
club and the city, it was also a pivotal moment in British
history. A time of change, of class barriers being vaulted
over, of liberation, even rebellion. Plums in mouths
shrank or were swallowed as regional accents swarmed
all over the BBC. Hair became longer, skirts shorter,
music louder and played to a different beat. There
was a swing to the left politically too, with a Labour
government and a Prime Minister with a Liverpool
seat. Suddenly, life itself seemed to be played to a
different beat. Shackles and knickers were coming off
and crowds began singing at football grounds. But if
there was a hint of Yankee behind The Beatles, football
songs in Liverpool were strictly homegrown. Certain
teams and individuals were targeted, but the words were

often impromptu and scrawled on beer mats before kick-off.

When it came to 'lyrics', no one could compare with Shanks. And the 'exaggeration' that had enlivened long nights in the Glenbuck cottage was an integral part of the package. Whether talking up the team or dismembering opponents, he would conjure expressions that could make players either crack up or cringe. But, when delivered in that James Cagney staccato, they brooked no argument. Those on the wrong end wished they were wearing a bulletproof vest.

Even at Grimsby, players said they 'felt two inches taller' under him. At Huddersfield, Ray Wilson remembered: 'We players looked forward to team meetings. It was like a comedy half-hour, it was wonderful. He never mentioned the opposition in detail but would just talk. "We're at home to Lincoln. One-horse race. We'll get a point at Walsall, then Grimsby at home. No bother." By the time he'd finished, we'd be unbeaten for the next six weeks and in third place! He staggered me; I couldn't believe that anybody could be so besotted by just one thing … He deserved Liverpool, and they deserved him.'

The pivotal signings of Yeats and St John saw Shankly at his persuasive best – he had threatened to resign if they flopped. And when Yeats expressed doubts about joining 'a Division Two outfit', he was informed: 'We're in the Second Division this season but next season we'll be in the First.' It was said with the certainty that night follows day.

It was the same line Shanks had pedalled to George Scott, whose family in Scotland had doubts about their boy joining. Now 76, Scott has memories of Shanks on instant recall, and says: 'He was a simple man, a miner, yet he could always find the right words. But it wasn't just the words, it was the total conviction in the way he delivered them that had the effect. Another thing he said to me was, "You're like the cornerstone of the Anglican Cathedral. Nobody ever sees it but without it the cathedral doesn't get built." He was referring to the fact that I was one of his first signings. I don't know how he thought these things up, or whether they were off the cuff, but he knew how to deal with people. Shanks had an aura about him. You always felt his presence even before you saw him. He had a way of building you up.'

This was never more evident than when he signed Peter Thompson from Preston. Noticing the crowds gathering at Anfield on a weekday, the young flier asked: 'Is there somebody famous coming?' Shanks, never one to miss an open goal, told him: 'Aye son, you. I'm going to make you the greatest player of all time. You'll be so fast, you'll catch pigeons, you'll be a great tackler, a great header of the ball, the fastest player in England.' Thompson would be yet another to realise that resistance was futile. He repeated what Yeats, St John, Scott and many others had said: 'You couldn't not sign for him.'

A youngster who desperately wanted to sign but was let go still sings his praises. David Kershaw CBE, JP, Hon D Ed, FRSA was a tall, gangly centre-half who had his dreams dashed by Shankly yet wrote a book to express his gratitude for being put on the right path. *Thanks, Shanks*, ghosted by Chris Arnot, reveals the astonishingly kind, caring side to a manager who had built his reputation as a tough guy. Kershaw, now 77 and a distinguished educationalist still dealing with failing schools, recalls: 'I was a big, dirty centre-half but missed a tackle in the Northern Intermediate League and the centre-forward ran through and scored. Shankly told me: "You're a nice lad but not quite good enough. Give me a day or two and I'll get you a job." For a couple of days, I was heartbroken, but I went back, and he said: "I've got you a job at Marks & Spencer filling shelves. But we've watched you with others and think you've got it in you to be a teacher." I told him I do enjoy talking to players, but I said: "Mr Shankly, can I tell you something? I've never said this before, but I can hardly read or write." I'd failed my 11-plus and left school at 14. He said: "Leave it with me."

'Two days later he'd fixed it up with M&S Bradford and gave me £50 in notes – a huge amount in those days. He said: "I've got you a tutor who will help you with your English." Lo and behold, that's what happened. It took me five attempts, but I got English 'O' level thanks to the tutoring. That was how he changed my life – I became a head teacher. He paid for it out of his own pocket and he did it for the next 12 months. I was no longer attached to the club and I'd go and see him, and he did it again – another £50. I was just one of many young men who he took the trouble to do that for. And that sums up the nature of the man. I didn't realise at the time that he was an old-fashioned socialist. He cared about people. The way in which he motivated us was amazing. When I was with him, I was the most important person in the world. I don't know how he did it as he wasn't over-articulate or over-flowery. He just said it as it was.'

Shankly had left school at the same tender age and hadn't had the benefit of a tutor yet possessed something close to genius for finding the right words. He was just as articulate whether lifting his own players or demolishing opponents. According to Scott, he wanted to turn Anfield into a fortress and he recalls: 'He took me and my dad out on to the pitch and proudly said, "This place will become a bastion of invincibility and you are very lucky, young man, to be here. They will all come here and be beaten, son." Those are words I will never forget.'

When it comes to belittling opponents, nothing beats the tale George Best put in his book as told to him by Ray Clemence. It goes like this: 'Before a Liverpool-United game, Shankly had received the United team sheet and he incorporated it into his team talk,' wrote Best. 'His intention was to run us down and, in so doing, boost the confidence of his own players. "Alex Stepney," Shanks began. "A flapper of a goalkeeper. Hands like a Teflon frying pan – non-stick. Right-back, Shay Brennan. Slow on the turn, give him a roasting. Left-back is Tony Dunne. Even slower than Brennan. He goes on an overlap at twenty past three and doesn't come back until a quarter to four. Right-half, Nobby Stiles. A dirty little ****. Kick him twice as hard as he kicks you and you'll have no trouble with him. Bill Foulkes, a big, cumbersome centre-half who can't direct his headers. He has a head like a sheriff's badge, so play on him. Paddy Crerand," he said, "slower than steam rising off a dog turd. You'll bypass him easily."

'Liverpool's players felt as if they were growing in stature with his every word. "David Sadler," Shanks continued. "Wouldn't get a place in our reserves. And finally, John Aston. A chicken, hit him once and you'll never hear from him again." As the manager finished his demolition job on United, Emlyn Hughes raised his hand. "That's all very well, boss," he said, "but you haven't mentioned George Best, Denis Law or Bobby Charlton." Shanks turned on him and growled: "You mean to tell me we cannae beat a team with only three players in it?"'

Like that other irrepressible motormouth of the day, Muhammad Ali, Shanks's quips were often blindingly simple yet oozed originality. And like Ali, who had corner man Bundini Brown feeding him the punchlines, the unlikely Boot Room Oscar Wilde was Paisley. 'He used to steal my lines,' said the Geordie, but only occasionally. Most were Shankly originals and as *Daily Express* Merseyside correspondent John Keith aptly put it: 'He was always on stage. We were all Boswells, waiting for the words to drop out of his mouth.' Another scribe to come under his spell was James Lawton. He wrote in *The Independent*: 'Bill Shankly's life was a torrent of often eccentric commitment, and no one ever doubted that at its heart was one drive above all others. It was to defend and celebrate the game that had brought so much joy and purpose to his life.'

The commitment often extended to five-a-side games with youngsters after training; the eccentricity was that he and Paisley, even in middle age, would play as if the World Cup was hanging on them. They said the old brigade never lost and weren't above 'cheating' to preserve their record. 'Silent Knight' Chris Lawler figures in one of these classic Shankly cameos. It happened in a game at Melwood when the manager claimed to have scored the decisive goal, the 'posts' being rolled-up jumpers. But the kids hotly disputed it so Lawler, who had limped off with a knock, was called upon to give his verdict. 'Chris,' boomed Shankly, 'you're an honest man. Was that a goal?' Lawler shook his head and said: 'Sorry Boss, it didn't go in.' Shankly was aghast. He quipped: 'Jesus Christ, Chris, you haven't uttered a word in five years and when you do you tell a bloody lie.'

Shanks admitted that he came to Liverpool 'for the potential', as he knew 'the Kop were dying to have a team to support'. He certainly gave them one – several – and so much more. His magic really did rub off on others and on the fans, too. Word soon got around that you could go to his house for his autograph and end up getting invited in for tea. He lived in a modest semi-detached on Bellefield Avenue, West Derby. The once-neat front garden had to be paved over to cope with the invading hordes. Stories were legion about how the manager would get tickets for people, discuss the game and could be a soft touch for a hard-luck story. On trains to and from matches, fans would engage him in conversation. Or he would engage them. Even outings with his family could be taken over by fans wanting to chat, while holidays in St Anne's or Blackpool would see him in beachside kickabouts with waiters.

There were also stories of how, some 15 minutes before kick-off, there would be no sign of the manager. Then the dressing room door would burst open. As the team were lacing up their boots, their leader would appear – dishevelled, shirt torn, hair tousled, tie all over the place. Decades before the term 'crowd-surfing' was coined, he had been doing it on the Kop. Unable to find a way through that impenetrable sardine tin of humanity, he had been lifted up by Kopites and passed along above their heads as kids used to be to get to the front. He had gone there to talk football, but they just wanted to share him around. This was his communion with the Kop and theirs with him.

It may seem trite to canonise such behaviour, but what of his most famous quote of all? A throwaway line delivered tongue-in-cheek yet 'football is more important than life and death' is integral to the debate about the game being a substitute for religion. Then Archbishop of Canterbury, George Carey, even used it in an address. And academics often haggle over it. In his paper *Mourning and loss: Finding meaning in the mourning for Hillsborough,* Michael Brennan writes:

'It is often stated elsewhere that football functions as a surrogate religion. To say that football matters and functions in this light in Liverpool is to understate its significance. Asked in 1985 if football matters too much in Liverpool, former deputy leader of the city council, Derek Hatton, an Evertonian, quipped: "It's like asking mice if they cared too much about cheese."'

Shanks would have loved that. But he would have railed against 'surrogate'. He said: 'I have to invent another word to fully describe the Anfield spectators. It is more than fanaticism, it's a religion. To the many thousands who come here to worship, Anfield isn't a football ground, it's a sort of shrine. These people are not simply fans, they're more like members of one extended family.'

He, of course, was their god. Brennan compares him with legendary American baseball player Joe DiMaggio, who is celebrated in song by Simon and Garfunkel. According to Brennan, the famous lines in 'Mrs Robinson': 'Where have you gone, Joe DiMaggio/A nation turns its lonely eyes to you', 'evokes a sense of nostalgia for an age of lost American innocence'. It's much the way Hillsborough mourners looked to Shanks who, although long gone, was a father figure the mention of whose name could give comfort to the grieving. If that was a period of real-life tragedy, the near death of the club itself two decades later provoked similar yearnings. No name was revered and mentioned more than Shankly's when Hicks and Gillett took Liverpool to the brink.

It was bad enough that they had damaged the club, but the contempt they showed for the values he had lived by is what made them hate figures. 'Sacrilege' is an oft-used word to describe what the pair did to Liverpool FC and its congregation. And it's no coincidence that the fans' first union, born amid the darkest days, was called Spirit of Shankly. Fans were crying out for a return to his values, especially as other predators lurked in the undergrowth. And those values are exactly what SOS has been fighting for (notwithstanding an upturn on the field) with another group of American capitalists at the helm. As for those who met at the Sandon pub to form that union, you just know Shanks would have given them an inspirational speech, not to mention his full-throated blessing.

Wrapped up in the nostalgia argument is that Shanks's reign also coincided with better times generally. Harold Wilson, whose constituency was Huyton, presided over a time of optimism, full employment and good humour. And those three essentials for civic harmony haven't always been in evidence since Shanks died. Whether Heysel and Hillsborough, industrial meltdown or league title drought, it was a time of considerable angst until the recent resurgence. On Merseyside, there has been a huge loss – of life, of jobs, of income, of pre-eminence in football. Only in the last three years – and early 2014 – has the football been a galvanising force at least for the Red half. Not least because of a return to the Liverpool Way in working as a team and with the manager building a rapport with the fans and thus evoking comparisons with Shanks himself.

'The will to restore the past following loss is a universal principle of human psychology,' argues Brennan. And Shanks's appeal, like DiMaggio's, lies not only in his iconic status but a longing for times when all seemed well with the world. The pseudo-religious aspect was most graphically depicted at Shanks's last competitive game. At the FA Cup Final of 1974, two fans ran on to the hallowed turf and kissed Shanks's feet. And what of my otherwise-agnostic Malaysian friend who calls visiting Anfield 'doing the haj' and watching a big game 'high mass'?

There have been countless examples where football can be seen as a substitute for religion, many of them long after Shankly's passing. Most notable was post-Hillsborough when, according to the memorial edition of the *Liverpool Echo*, 'Anfield became Liverpool's third cathedral as around a million pilgrims flocked to pay tribute to the Hillsborough dead.' But post-Shanks players such as Robbie Fowler, Steven Gerrard and Jamie Carragher have all been subjected to varying degrees of deification. The irony is rich, as Shankly wasn't religious at all but saw socialism as a substitute.

The 60s were the defining decade of the 20th century and the sense of emancipation wasn't confined to Britain. It was a decade of famous movements, notably peace and civil rights, but also fashion and social. It was a decade of famous names, of epochal events, of turmoil and transformation. It was a decade of wars, assassinations and moon landings. Few decades have had the impact of the 60s, and Shankly's tenure as Liverpool manager, which stretched from 1959 to 1974, encompassed it all.

It was also the defining period in Liverpool FC's history. The events of that era moved and shook the world; Shankly moved and shook Liverpool FC. As an Austin A40 driver, he's not often compared to an F1 mogul, but it was hard not to think of him when Enzo Ferrari called himself 'an agitator of men'. And when asked what his favourite Ferrari was, the Italian answered: 'The one that has yet to be built.' Substitute 'player' for 'Ferrari' and 'born' for 'built', and it could have been the great football man speaking.

Chapter 9

'I want to build a team that's invincible, so they have to send a team from bloody Mars to beat us.'

Bill Shankly

SHANKS'S AMBITION had always been for Liverpool to become champions. Of England, of Europe, of the solar system ... and those bloody Martians would have to change their red strip if they came anywhere near Anfield. Finishing eighth in their first season back in the top flight in 1962/63 was seen as consolidation in some quarters but not by Shanks. 'Consolidate' was one of those words he would have had banned from the dictionary along with a few others that are a fixed bayonet short of annihilation. Nor did it tell the whole story. Three early home defeats before the leaves had fallen meant Nessie's cooker was sporting an unseasonal gleam but were a harsh reminder that they were operating at a higher level. They recovered well enough to harbour thoughts of the title before the season petered out. Still, Liverpool were building. Solid foundations. Spine. And putting some pretty tasty flesh on the bones. Yeats and St John had more than lived up to the manager's expectations. And, after a slow start, so had another Scot, Willie Stevenson. But it wasn't just the big money buys that were delivering – the youth system was too, with Lawrence, Lawler, Byrne, Smith and Callaghan all emerging as first-team regulars. No one expected them to be eighth next season.

A dead giveaway that Shanks was getting close to the team he wanted came when he signed a contract – the first of his career. He had always worked without one, saying: 'If I cannot do the job, it is up to the people who employ me to do as they wish.' But under pressure from the board, who were terrified of losing him, he finally agreed to put pen to paper. They shouldn't have worried; ever since he arrived, he had been putting 'Anfield' as his address on any bit of paper shoved in front of him – even hotel registration forms.

He would also make only one significant addition to the squad. The aforementioned Peter Thompson cost just £37,000 in a deal Shanks hailed as 'daylight robbery'. A mazy dribbler with a goal in him, Thompson would be the major beneficiary of the rediscovered laser in Stevenson's left boot. He would add pace, power and a box of tricks to Liverpool's already formidable arsenal. Although lacking a headline-grabbing superstar, they had no real weakness and, above all else, were a team. They ground out top spot against some formidable opponents, but none were a match for the Reds, who were literally willed to the title by the Kop and its chief conductor.

It was only their second season back in the top flight and it felt like something momentous was happening. When Arsène Wenger challenged Manchester United's hegemony around the millennium, he spoke of a change in the balance of power. What Shanks was doing was delivering a new football superpower and, like Wenger, he was introducing new methods and new thinking. Tommy Lawrence's son Steve recalls: 'Shanks was ahead of his time when it came to training. I remember my dad telling me Shanks had said, "Why are you running on roads – you don't play on them." He brought in footballs from the start of training and made sure he had the best people around him that were good for the club and the team.'

But perhaps the biggest change was with the goalkeeper. Says Steve Lawrence: 'Shanks made my dad the first sweeper-keeper as he wanted to play a high line to stop the forwards coming through, which he did to good effect. In those days, of course, goalkeepers could pick up back passes so didn't really play out with their feet. I think Shanks would have wanted his keepers to get it out to players quickly and let them pass it like in today's game.' The back-pass rule wasn't changed until 1992 – 18 years after Shanks retired.

Roger Hunt put the success down to fitness, but others felt it was team spirit and desire. They were all equals, on equal pay and fought for each other. It was a strange season, though, and they lost 11 games – ten more than they lost in 2018/19! At times it seemed that no one wanted to win the title. But no one wanted it more than Shanks, and when it was finally secured, he said it was his 'greatest moment in football'. It wouldn't be his last.

How to follow it was the question. Anyone expecting a flotilla of signings would have been disappointed. Shanks knew his men were worthy champions – they could go on to 'conquer the bloody world' in his eyes. And the only addition was the versatile Geoff Strong for £40,000 from Arsenal. His arrival suggested Shanks was already planning for Europe. He had won the title with 14 players, two of whom had played four games between them, and there were no substitutes back then. He wanted players who could play in more than one position.

As champions, Liverpool had a lot on their plate, and a close-season tour of the United States was the last thing they needed. Not even a visit to Chicago, haunt of his gangster heroes and Soldier Field, where Jack Dempsey fought Gene Tunney, could make up for the disruption. It wasn't helped by Shanks's eccentric refusal to adhere to local times. Indeed, Shankly blamed their transatlantic jaunt for the injuries his players were to suffer in the new campaign. 'They didnae have enough rest,' he maintained before a more demanding season all round. Europe would be a huge adventure but there was also the FA Cup. Hard though it is to grasp today, the old trophy carried enormous kudos in Shanks's day. And Liverpool had never won it. Evertonians used to say the Liver Birds would fly away if they did. The Reds had won six league titles but of the cup they had had only a couple of sniffs – as runners-up in 1914 and 1950. Shanks knew that immortality would be his if he could finally land the elusive prize for Liverpool. But even more than that, he knew how much it meant to the fans.

Liverpool were one of the cup favourites in 1964/65 but seldom looked like getting those Liver Birds off their moorings. Making hard work of every round, they needed a replay against little Stockport. It was the first game Shanks missed (to go on a spying mission in Europe) and he refused to believe the result when told. But the Reds survived and somehow made it to Wembley to meet Leeds in a rain-sodden final. George Scott, unofficial 12th man, even though there were no subs, remembers walking on to that glistening greensward before the game. 'The Kop were already in full voice and Shanks turned to Bob Paisley and said, "We just can't let these people down. We just can't."'

Three minutes after kick-off, it looked for all the world as if they would. Left-back Gerry Byrne broke his collarbone in a collision with Bobby Collins. The cup final injury jinx had struck early and still there were no substitutes. Shanks had two options: he could either bring Byrne off or strap him up as a passenger at the mercy of the Leeds hard men. He chose neither. He knew Byrne was a tough nut and he told him to carry on ... without strapping. 'Leeds might not notice,' he whispered to Bob Paisley. They didn't. In a piece of uncommon valour akin to Bert Trautmann's in 1956, Byrne played on. Holding his arm gingerly (if you looked closely) across his chest, he was still able to run – and tackle and pass – albeit in agony. Not just for 87 minutes but 117, plus injury time. And in a plot at which Hollywood might have drawn the line, it was Byrne, on an overlapping run in extra time, who provided the cross for Hunt to head home. It looked for all the world like the winner – only for Billy Bremner to equalise. The travelling Kop seemed to flinch in unison. But as they wondered who was writing the script, the Saint (Ian St John) came to the rescue with a spectacular winner. Cue bedlam beneath the twin towers and in the Red half of Merseyside. Was there a flapping of wings? If the Liver Birds had taken flight, like Leeds with Byrne's injury, no one would have noticed.

The next day's celebrations more than matched those for VE Day and the Relief of Mafeking, claimed the local media. The crowd that welcomed the team home was put at over 250,000. They crawled up buildings, clung to lamp posts, window ledges, rooftops and each other in scenes not matched until the Champions League parade in 2019. Fans descended on the centre of Liverpool like bees on their favourite hive. The *Liverpool Daily Post* wrote: 'It made the recent Beatles reception look like a Vicarage tea party.' Agog at the sheer scale of it, Shanks for once allowed the magnitude of what he had achieved to sink in – and it reduced the tough guy to tears. He said it was his greatest day in football – another one.

It didn't turn out so well for Scott though. When he went back to his digs, he recalls finding 'a letter from the club waiting for me from Mr Shankly. I opened it thinking that I had been permanently promoted to the first-team squad and that 1966 would be my big breakthrough year. I was brought right back to reality when the letter stated I had been placed on the transfer list. On the Monday morning I barged into Shanks's office distraught. He could see I was upset, and he came round from his desk and put his arm round me. "George, I'll give you five good reasons why you should leave this club. Five: Callaghan, Hunt, St John, Smith and Thompson. If you want to progress, it's time to go. But I want you to always remember that at this particular time you are the 12th-best player in the world. Now go back to Aberdeen and prove it."'

It's a moot point whether Shankly, knowing the board were letting Scott go, deliberately made him 12th man in the cup final to soften the coming blow. Scott had gone into the office devastated and received confirmation of what he had dreaded yet had come out feeling ten feet tall.

Liverpool were still in Europe and faced the might of Inter Milan two nights later. If the FA Cup campaign had been a grind, the European Cup had been quite the opposite. And although a rookie in continental football, Shanks had plenty of opportunities to show what he was made of. After an 11-1 aggregate romp against KR Reykjavík came Anderlecht, and it was during the build-up to meeting the Belgians that Shanks produced one of his psychological masterstrokes. After getting Ron Yeats to try an all-red strip, Shanks felt it would make his players 'look two inches taller' and more intimidating. 'We'll frighten the life out of them,' he added. And so, Liverpool's all-red kit was born. Frightened or not, Anderlecht surrendered 3-0 at Anfield and the All-Reds were able to steal the return 1-0 to proceed to a three-match, 42-day epic against Cologne. It ended in a coin toss and even that needed a 'replay', the chosen disc getting stuck on its edge in the mud. Yeats called correctly but Shanks was less than ecstatic. Disgusted at the way a big game had been decided, he earned universal plaudits for attempting to console a distraught Cologne bench.

And so, to the semi-final against the defending champions, Inter Milan. It was the night when the din could have been heard across the Irish Sea, according to old-timers. Gates were closed at 5.30pm and the Kop was already in full voice. Hours before kick-off the noise was deafening, the ground in tumult. But Shanks stoked it another notch. He ordered Byrne, who by then had had his arm put in a sling, and Milne, who had missed the final altogether, to parade the FA Cup just as the Italians took the field. If the timing was worthy of the Philharmonic Hall, the decibels were of a far heavier metal – and had the desired effect. Visibly shaken and with their eardrums around their ankles, the erstwhile masters of *catenaccio* didn't know what had hit them. A rampant Liverpool tore into them to score three times. Inter did manage one though – through a rare Yeats slip

– but Shankly was sure the advantage was big enough; he thought Inter were down and out. He underestimated the depths to which they would sink in the return and the away goal was the least of his worries.

The stitch-up started the night before the game. An all-night cacophony worthy of Dante, church bells and car horns combined to prevent the Liverpool party from sleeping. The San Siro was a cauldron of hate and a smoke-bomb was thrown at the Liverpool bench. The All-Reds needed a lot more than 'two inches' of height. They soon found themselves 2-0 down to highly controversial goals and when St John pulled 'one' back, it was disallowed for no apparent reason. The Liverpool bench were smouldering once again, but they sensed there was no way they would be allowed to win here; the final was to be played in the same stadium.

The video doesn't show a stonewall case for larceny and there was no argument about Inter's third, but you can see why the Reds felt cheated. Every decision went against them. However, it was after the game that the evidence really mounted. As they left the field, Tommy Smith lost the plot and hacked down the referee! What amazed Smith was that Spaniard Ortiz de Mendibil simply picked himself up and trotted off; no eye contact and no sending off. An investigation by the *Sunday Times* – not UEFA – would find that this was prime time for Inter's match-fixing period, and several other clubs suffered similar fates. If Ortiz de Mendibil had been got at, he took it to his grave.

Chapter 10

'My new team is going to go off like a great bomb in the sky.'

Bill Shankly

THEY SAY the true measure of a man is shown in adversity. Well, by any standards, being done like an Italian kipper *was* adversity. Stinking, gut-wrenching, faith-destroying adversity. The English champions had almost certainly been cheated – and just when they thought they were within sight of the ultimate prize. A similar scenario had put paid to Borussia Dortmund's hopes a year earlier. If Shanks now had two candidates jousting for his 'greatest moment in football', there would only ever be one that stood glaringly unopposed as his worst.

It hit Shanks hard. Defeat he could take but this was the very antithesis of the values he had been brought up to believe in – in a village where no one locked their doors. Asked in a TV interview how he would like to be remembered, he said: 'Basically as an honest man in a game that is sometimes short on honesty. That I've been working honestly for the people of Liverpool to try and give them entertainment.' Honesty, he felt in his marrow, had been in very short supply in Italy. From the hotel where they couldn't sleep to the match they couldn't win. 'No team in the world can beat Liverpool 3-0,' he had told his players in the dressing room immediately afterwards. 'They must have been drugged up to the eyeballs and the referee was bribed.'

Pun intended, there was plenty of substance behind the first claim. In 2010 an Italian court upheld ex-Inter striker Ferruccio Mazzola's allegation of systematic use of illegal or performance-enhancing drugs under the Inter regime of Angelo Moratti in the mid-to-late 60s. Inter's failure to appeal was regarded as proof of guilt. Earlier investigations by the *Sunday Times* showed that match-fixing was also rife, although several key witnesses, including referees, died before it could be proved beyond reasonable doubt. No one of a Liverpool persuasion had any doubt.

But with the jeers of mocking fans piercing his ears as they were driven away from the stadium, Shanks knew he couldn't allow this bitterness to fester. It was only just over a fortnight since they had made history and he couldn't let anything take the glory away from winning the FA Cup. Or diminish the euphoria of those victorious scenes at Wembley and back in Liverpool. Not for the players nor the people. This could have put a massive – albeit retrospective – dampener on those parades, but Shanks wasn't going to allow it to happen.

Even if it would affect him – some say he was haunted by it – he wouldn't permit any sense of grievance, however justified, to spoil their finest hour, their summer break or the following season.

The irony was that amid the catcalls, the whistles and the gloating, Liverpool were showered with glowing praise from Herrera, the Inter coach, of all people. 'They are one of the best teams in the world,' said the Argentine. Easy to say when you've won, of course, but sickening to hear when you've lost in such circumstances. Shanks must have wondered whether Herrera was twisting the knife but, still searching for a positive, he listened. Realising he had been helpless against the sinister forces at work – there was no stopping the *Nerazzurri* back then and they duly retained their trophy – he seized an opportunity. Excruciating though it must have been, he turned Herrera's praise and Inter's wild celebrations into a mark of how far his team had progressed. He addressed his players once more and this time he told them: 'All right, we've lost. But see what you've done. Inter Milan are the unofficial champions of the world, and all these people are going mad because they are so pleased they beat Liverpool. That's the standard you have raised yourselves up to.' It was one of the hardest things he ever had to do; he was a fully paid-up firebrand yet this, in turning the other cheek, was worthy of a Buddhist monk. Among his many qualities, he was a fast learner.

There was still plenty to shout about from a season in which they had ended a 73-year FA Cup drought and reached the semis in their first foray in the European Cup. And what bigger confidence vote could he give the team than sticking with them for the following campaign; he didn't feel the need to buy a single player even though they were back in Europe in the Cup Winners' Cup. There was absolutely no panic but there was a subtle change in tactics.

Even though 'defence' was another of his unmentionable words, Shanks would make it his priority in away ties on the continent. *Catenaccio* it wasn't, nor was it parking the bus, but it was containment of sorts – a tactic that would be successfully employed by two other British managers better known for their flair – Alex Ferguson and Brian Clough, not to mention Jürgen Klopp. And it worked – most notably against Juventus in the Cup Winners' Cup when Liverpool went 1-0 down late in the away first leg, only to sit back to avoid conceding a second. They duly turned over the Old Lady 2-0 at Anfield in the return. Herrera would have approved.

The biggest game, inevitably billed as the Battle of Britain, was the semi-final against Jock Stein's Celtic. Liverpool prevailed after a titanic tussle and this was the same Celtic that would become the first British club to win the European Cup in 1967. No one knew that then and there was no reason to suggest that Shanks's Liverpool wouldn't get the honour. But when Celtic lifted the trophy in Lisbon, Shanks told his friend: 'John, you're immortal.' It was a generous thing to say, especially when he had eyed that slice of immortality for himself – and Celtic's vanquished opponents were none other than Inter Milan.

The year before Celtic's success it had been a shock when the Reds didn't pick up the Cup Winners' Cup at Hampden Park but Liverpool had already taken care of the main business – they were league champions once again and by a comfortable six points. It was perhaps an even more worthy triumph than before as the competition had stepped up. It was expected to herald the arrival of a succession of trophies, but it wasn't to be.

Everyone knows that Paisley would win more than Shanks, that the 70s and 80s would see an even greater period of dominance than the 60s.

But it's often overlooked that this new Liverpool era would actually experience a mini trophy-drought. Where Shanks stood steadfastly by his well-oiled machine, rivals went out and bought new and sleeker models. United finally had the support cast for the Holy Trinity of Best, Charlton and Law, while Manchester City boasted their own stellar trio in Franny Lee, Mike Summerbee and Colin Bell. They also benefitted from the inspired partnership of Joe Mercer and Malcolm Allison. Revie had acquired Allan Clarke to sniff out goals but for the most part Leeds were still being Leeds. But at the end of the 60s Liverpool were no longer quite Liverpool. That title triumph in the 1965/66 season was as good as it got for a while.

The following campaign the Reds would slip to fifth place and had to endure another difficult night in

Europe. Few saw a threat from second-round opponents, Ajax Amsterdam, and no one in England had heard of a wiry 19-year-old inside-forward by the name of Johan Cruyff. But in a game that Shankly swore should never have been played because of fog, Liverpool lost their way and crashed 5-1. Poor visibility was a factor but what was clear for all to see was that Ajax were an emerging force and Cruyff was something special.

Shanks's defiant 'we'll beat them 5-0 at Anfield' cry drew a full, expectant house but could only inspire a 2-2 draw in the return. The consensus was that the great team was ageing and needed rebuilding. And criticism that Shanks had left the job too late isn't just based on hindsight. Yeats and St John were aware of it at the time but if anyone should know if the great man had a weakness, it was Paisley. He would later say: 'If Bill had one failing, it was that he did not like to upset the players that had done so well for him. He was a softie at heart.'

The one signing he did make that season was Emlyn Hughes for £65,000 from Blackpool. A future England captain and Liverpool legend, Hughes was just the kind of dynamic, versatile young player needed to re-energise the squad. It was another deal that Shanks called 'daylight robbery', but he was now on a spree worthy of his gangster heroes. Another fledgling star was Ray Clemence for just £18,000 from Scunthorpe but he didn't go straight into the first-team squad.

Two more expensive buys, Tony Hateley for £96,000 (July 1967) and Alun Evans for £110,000

(September 1968) would disappoint. They were meant to complement each other but injuries and a lack of confidence combined to stem their progress. Both would be sold off at a considerable loss as the great Red machine had hit a rut. Busby's United won the league in 1966/67 and followed Celtic in winning the European Cup the next year. City won the league in 1967/68 when Liverpool endured another fallow season and Everton were champions in 1969/70. That season Liverpool lost to Watford in an FA Cup quarter-final. It marked the end of an era for Yeats, St John, Byrne and Lawrence – four of Shanks's mainstays and old favourites. He told them: 'Right, that's it. A lot of you have just played your last game for Liverpool.'

Sadly, none of them got the 'George Scott' treatment and some – St John, and also Hunt – felt they were harshly dealt with. The problem was that Shanks had 'expected them to go on forever – like Peter Pan', said Nessie – and he found it very difficult to tell them otherwise. Not forever, but he had always believed players were at their peak between 28 and 33, and these players still had some of their best years left. Or so he thought.

He simply hadn't expected to have to rebuild so soon. He wasn't being cruel to be kind either – he just wasn't very good at saying goodbye to such loyal servants. He loved these players and he hated parting with them. As with players who got injured, he somehow felt let down – this time by the ageing process. He found it easier to deal with the Scotts and even the Kershaws than his 'heroes' – for the four in question were nothing less than that. He was as uncertain in dealing with the end of their careers as he had been sure-footed at the beginning.

Was he losing his touch? Not when it came to spotting players and he was at his best when looking at those from the lower leagues. In addition to Hughes and Clemence, in came Larry Lloyd (Bristol Rovers), Alec Lindsay (Bury), John Toshack (Cardiff), Steve Heighway (non-league Skelmersdale), along with Brian Hall from the youth ranks. He was on his way to building the next great Liverpool side. Was he confident of it working? James Lawton was one of a handful of journalists invited to hear his answer. He recalled in *The Independent*: 'Once, when he was explaining how he was going to re-make Liverpool after the fading of St John and Yeats, he clambered on to the desk in his little office beneath the old main stand. He stood on the table, on the balls of his feet, and then made a fist and raised it above his head. He said: "My new team is going to go off like a great bomb in the sky."'

New decade, new hope but the first season of the 70s turned out to be another nearly one for Liverpool. There was yet another different title winner – this time Arsenal – and the fifth since Liverpool's triumph in 1965/66. The Gunners would do the Double by beating Liverpool in the FA Cup Final after having already clinched the First Division title. Shankly's 'new' team also failed narrowly in the Fairs Cup, going down to Leeds, but it was a season of promise, not least for the signing of a certain Kevin Keegan for £33,000 from Scunthorpe. 'Robbery with violence' was how Shanks described this one.

Nope, Shanks had lost neither his touch nor his tongue. Even for top players who turned Liverpool down, he had a telling riposte. After Alan Ball chose Everton, he told him: 'Don't worry, Alan. At least you'll be able to play *close* to a great team.' He was similarly disappointed when Lou Macari opted for Manchester United, but insisted: 'I only wanted him for the reserves anyway.'

By now, more than a decade in the role of football manager, favourite uncle and national institution, he could still drive a team and work a crowd. And the crowd hadn't lost their love for him. Whether you were a student of the game or a stand-up comedian, his words – still delivered in a rapid-fire way – were irresistible. But it was those he came up with on the steps of St George's Hall after that FA Cup defeat to Arsenal that have gone down in history.

It had been a heartbreaking loss but still half of Merseyside was there to welcome the Liverpool players home. So, Shanks had to tell the people something. A flimsy grasp of world affairs was no impediment to chiming with the mood of the time. On the open-top bus trip from Lime Street station, Shanks turned to university-educated winger Hall and asked: 'Son, you know about these things, who is that chairman with the red book and lots of sayings? The Chinaman, what's his name?' A bemused Hall answered: 'Is it Chairman Mao you mean?' To which Shanks replied: 'Aye, that's him son, Chairman Mao, that's him.'

Minutes later, in front of that grand neo-classic building, Shanks addressed the multitude. 'Ladies and gentlemen,' he said, 'yesterday at Wembley we may have lost the cup, but you the people have won everything ... you have conquered. You have won over the policemen in London. You won over the London public and it's questionable if Chairman Mao of China could have arranged such a show of strength as you have shown yesterday and today. Defeat? What is that? A detail brothers and sisters, a footnote in the struggle for supremacy. We. You and Me. Liverpool. Together we can conquer the world. Since I've come to Anfield I've drummed it into my players, time and again, that it is a privilege to play for you people. If they didn't believe me then, they do now.'

He had seized the moment yet again. The 'speech' lasted only a couple of minutes but still resonates. It became known as 'the Chairman Mao speech' but the words belong more to Martin Luther King than the Chinese leader. Indeed, in terms of bonding with the people of Liverpool, it was right out of 'I have a dream'. They were already his people and the speech would come to define him – even if the dream had already been realised years ago. They had lost and had gone five years without a trophy yet a quarter of a million were still eating out of his hand.

Chapter 11

'I'm only looking after the shop until a proper manager arrives.'

Bob Paisley

IF DISMANTLING his beloved 60s team broke Shanks's heart, assembling the bold, new 70s side would reboot his love affair – with Liverpool, with football, with life – his permanent podium of priorities. Even in defeat at the 1971 FA Cup Final, he was more like his old, incorrigible self. It was a new decade, a new era and he had exciting new players. But the turning of the page in football lagged infuriatingly adrift of the calendar.

Shanks's two great teams came to be defined by their decades and, just like the side of the 60s, the next incarnation took a while to get going. But unlike their predecessors, once they did, the 70s side would go on and on ... until the 80s. The massive, incomprehensible, off-the-Richter shock was that Shanks didn't go with them.

There were many more pages to turn yet he slammed the book shut before he got anywhere near the end of the story. Or even the end of the decade. Having added yet more lustre to his legendary status by rebuilding to win the league, the FA Cup and, at long last, a European trophy, he quit. It was probably the worst news the city of Liverpool had had since Manchester built its Ship Canal and it caused widespread disbelief. Shanks's epic reign ended in the summer of 1974 – five days after West Germany stunned the Netherlands to win the World Cup and just weeks after his own final Wembley triumph – suddenly, shockingly, prematurely. It was nothing short of an abdication that no one, absolutely no one, saw coming.

He was just 60, fit enough to still play in five-a-sides. He had paraded his great new team and boasted of new triumphs – even a European conquest. He had crossed the threshold into a thrilling new era – even if he'd had to wait. In 1972 there had been yet another different name on the First Division trophy – Brian Clough's Derby County – who pipped both Leeds (second) and Liverpool (third on goal average) by just one point. But at least Shanks's men had taken them to the wire. And in 1973 the Reds won the league with three points to spare over runners-up Arsenal. They were the team of the season, of the decade, of the next decade.

In Keegan and Hughes, there were two new stars whose never-say-die approach on the field and ebullience off it were worthy of the manager himself. They quickly became his favourites. Keegan was a real Duracell man, a pocket rocket who could chase lost causes, harry, tackle, pass and score improbable goals. He was the perfect foil for a tall centre-forward like Toshack. The two developed an understanding on a par with Hunt and St John while augmenting the front two was the cultured Peter Cormack, an astute signing from Nottingham Forest. Behind this lethal attack, Hughes was also perpetual motion – and inspirational. In 1973, as well as getting Liverpool's name back on the league championship trophy, Shanks had finally got the hang of Europe. He won the UEFA Cup for a unique double. The two principal survivors and constants in the side from the 60s were the ageless Ian Callaghan and Tommy Smith. The pair were vital in ensuring that things were still done the Liverpool Way.

Behind the scenes, the club was sailing just as smoothly. They were now under the chairmanship of John Smith, a true captain of industry who ran breweries and an electronics firm as well as a tightly efficient ship at Anfield. Known as 'Dapper John' to locals, he still found time to chair the UK Sports Council for five years. There was no silly money, but Shanks didn't have to beg for funds if he wanted a player. Smith was determined to keep Liverpool at the forefront in Europe as well as at home. But his style was the yin to Shankly's yang. He once said: 'We are a very modest club. We don't talk. We don't boast. We are professional.' Shanks had got on better with previous chairmen, Tom Williams and Eric Roberts, but he couldn't deny that Smith knew what he was doing – he kept the ground up to scratch too, with the opening of a new main stand.

It was an era safely before the Premier League was even a twinkle, and you could still win the title with mere millionaires on the board. Six different champions in a row were testimony to an openness of competition that cannot even be conceived today. Life wasn't perfect – the Reds couldn't defend their trophy, coming second the following season to Leeds – but football was still more about football than the New York Stock Exchange. The Reds outclassed Newcastle in the final to win the FA Cup again and Shanks was worshipped more than ever. With a dynamic new team, the league and cup won in the last two years, a modern stadium, money for signings and a supportive board, there didn't seem to be a cloud on his horizon. He was even awarded the OBE.

But on 12 July 1974, Earth came off its axis for the Red half of Merseyside. Shanks's resignation was a full-blown JFK moment. Few believed it at first and many remember where they were when they heard the news. In those pre-mobile phone, pre-rolling news, prehistoric days, people asked strangers, called friends – several of them – and gathered around televisions in shop windows to check whether it was true. Players, directors, fans. But it *was* true. Shocking and inexplicable to everybody … but true. He'd had enough. The man who lived for Liverpool, the Scot who 'became' a Scouser, the most committed, charismatic man-manager and motivator of this or any era could no longer motivate himself. For 15 years, whenever people were in a dilemma, they had asked themselves: 'What would Shankly do?' Now it was: 'What has Shankly done?' And 'Why?'

Many refused to believe it. Even the board didn't get it. Players were dumbfounded. Hughes burst into tears. After all, wasn't 'retirement' on his list of banned words? If anyone was going to die with their steel-studded boots on it was Shanks. In the dugout. Shouting, urging, demanding his troops go on yet another offensive. A general in the heat of battle. JFK? There were more conspiracy theories about this than that business in Dallas. The only things missing were a book depository and a grassy knoll.

Shanks told the chairman he needed a break, wanted to spend more time with his wife and family, and make up for all those nights away scouting in some half-a-horse, lower league town. A break from carrying the aspirations of the fans on his shoulders, dealing with players who were beginning to get a bit uppity. Just a break. Very soon he spoke about not being finished in football and it looked as if a sabbatical might have served everyone better. It also emerged that he had half-heartedly offered to resign a couple of times before but had been talked out of it. On both occasions, Smith and club secretary Peter Robinson suggested he become general manager. But still wary of directors and mindful that he was very much a players' man, he had rejected the idea outright. The less he had to do with the board or paperwork, the better; he wanted to be out there on the grass, with the boys, breathing 'God's air'. Still.

He was, though, a bigger worrier than appearances suggested, and the weight of the job had taken its toll. His rhetoric had camouflaged his concerns; and his enthusiasm had hidden the enormity of the task. He worried about leaving players out of the team, let alone ending their careers. Now he was worrying about his own time and, yes, he did owe his long-suffering wife a few hundred nights in. For once doing right by Nessie, he was doing wrong by the club. He didn't leave them in the lurch – they were in an exceptionally healthy state thanks to him – but the surprise factor and the absence of a succession plan left the club shaken.

Unlike Alexander the Great, Shanks hadn't said 'to the strongest' when asked to whom his empire should go. In fact, it was left conspicuously unsaid. Anyway, it wasn't an empire. Nor was it a papacy or a royal family, although it may have felt like all three at times. It was a football club and a very special one, which *he* had made special. One of the reasons for that was the Boot Room but, as excellent as Messrs Paisley, Fagan and Bennett were, they were the support cast not the line of succession. Or so it was thought.

Leaving is hard to do – he'd had trouble asking players to leave, let alone himself. Yet the feeling, both at the time and now, with 46 years of hindsight, is that he might have handled it better, as could the club. Indeed, even today, the view persists that he could have been talked out of it. Paisley even offered to stand in for him while he took a break. But this time Shanks wasn't for turning – even if his words and actions betrayed a degree of ambivalence. In the *Shankly Speaks* recording, there was an element of bowing out at the top when he spoke of 'conquering Everest' and 'having no more points to prove'.

Yet the Monday after resigning on the Friday, he took training. A month later, he led the team out at Wembley for the Charity Shield. That was because Liverpool were having, what Robinson called 'a frightful time' trying to persuade Paisley to take over. Even when the former No.2 eventually did, he told the squad that he was 'only looking after the shop until a proper manager arrives'. The perennial Ian Callaghan, who played in midfield for the club between 1960 and 1978, said: 'Bob was very reluctant to become manager because he didn't think he was cut out for it. He was an introvert and preferred being in the background.'

Liverpool had just been warned of what can happen when a managerial legend becomes an unwitting spectre at his successor's feast. Manchester United thought they had done everything right by granting Shanks's old friend Busby an upstairs post, an office and a directorship when he retired. They had just been relegated. Sir Matt hadn't consciously interfered during the reigns of either Wilf McGuinness or Frank O'Farrell, but players had sought him out, nevertheless. Busby's mere presence had been enough to undermine them. Well aware of Shanks's irrepressible nature and the players' respect for him, Liverpool knew he would find it impossible not to get involved if given a similar post.

He had been to hell and back in deciding to walk away. He said: 'It was the most difficult thing in the world to make a decision like this and when I went to see the chairman, it was like walking to the electric chair.' Almost from the word go, there were suggestions that he had acted in haste and had immediately regretted it. A large part of him regretted it, of that there was no doubt. But he also owed Nessie big-time and had discussed it with her. He stuck to his decision. He also felt a certain bitterness towards the hierarchy. There were rumours of a rift with Smith who, some thought, preferred Paisley anyway – for a quieter life. Shanks was much closer to Robinson who, years later, would shake his head and say: 'I still don't know why.'

Even after Paisley had taken the reins, Shanks would still go to Melwood. He felt that was where he belonged. He went to train, to run around the perimeter, to keep fit, to remain a part of the scene that had been his life for 15 years. If it was understandable, it was an obvious interference with, if not an affront to, Paisley's authority and the beginning of a rift between the two. And when the club, desperate not to make things worse, gently suggested to Shanks that if he wanted to run around Melwood, he should do so in the afternoons, he took umbrage. It smacked of trying to bar Caesar from Rome and only added to his pain. He had a deep mistrust of the wealthy elite and thought he hadn't been given his due for building this great institution from 'the shambles' in which he had found it in 1959. In truth, if

they had given him the keys to Fort Knox, it wouldn't
have been nearly enough.

Chapter 12

'Retire is a terrible, silly word. They should get a new word for it. The only time you retire is when you're in a box and the flowers come out.'

Bill Shankly

THE FIRST post-Shankly season saw Liverpool trophy-less. According to Peter Robinson, Paisley struggled, especially with the media – but second place was no disaster. In truth, Shanks struggled a lot more in trying to come to terms with what he had done. Yes, he did 'resent' his treatment and 'felt shunned', according to biographer John Roberts. He had once said: 'Retire is a terrible, silly word. They should get a new word for it. The only time you retire is when you're in a box and the flowers come out. You can't retire because your mind will get sick. If you're bored with nothing to do, then you'll get sick.'

Shanks didn't have enough to do. Having given his life and soul, every fibre in his body and every synapse in his brain to football, he didn't have other pursuits to turn to. So, he ended up watching more games than ever. He also had a radio gig. And he kept fit … by training at Everton. Bellefield was almost next door but he had spent the last 15 years poking fun at them. In his definitive quotes bible, there's a chunky and disparaging chapter on the Blues, including: 'There are only two teams in Liverpool: Liverpool and Liverpool Reserves,' and 'If Everton were playing outside my bedroom window, I'd close the curtains.' Once when signing autographs at the Anfield players' entrance, he refused to sign in blue ink and had the kids scrambling for a pen of another colour. Then there's the one about him taking his dog for a walk and making sure it had done its business on Everton's practice pitches before returning home.

None of that stopped him from jogging around the place – he now took the dog on a different route – or even lending a hand. At least he felt welcome. 'I have been received more warmly by Everton than I have by Liverpool,' he said. He also watched the third Merseyside club, Tranmere Rovers, and gave plenty of advice to Toshack when he took the reins at Swansea. But it was 'a bit of this and a bit of that', which was nowhere near enough for a managerial colossus barely past his prime. Yesterday's genius, he most definitely wasn't – he had passed the ultimate test of reconstruction with a double first – the league and the UEFA Cup – and it's impossible not to think that he would have won a lot more if he had stayed.

In his biography, he wrote: 'I thought that if I was away from the pressures of Anfield for a while, and rested, it would make me fitter and rejuvenate me. I felt I could contribute more later on … I still wanted to help Liverpool because the club had become my life. But I wasn't given the chance.' Whilst underlining his anger, it begs the question: in what capacity could he have helped? Would being general manager have worked? It hadn't worked at United with Busby and nor did it at Blackburn with Kenny Dalglish 20 years later. Could he have managed another club? Unimaginable, perhaps, but being the gaffer – full-blown, hands-on – is what he did and all he knew. But how could he just transfer all that intensity to somewhere else? If a player had a knock on the knee would it be 'Tranmere's knee' or 'Swansea's knee'? These cracks had a Liverpool copyright. Yet a toned-down version may not have worked either. He had just been too good at it. He was an impossible act to follow – even for himself.

Any lingering thoughts of returning to Liverpool were soon dashed when Paisley, finally warming to the task, emulated Shanks by winning the league and the UEFA Cup the following season. The trophies – including the big one that Shanks never landed – rolled in with even greater frequency. The man who didn't consider himself 'a proper manager' became the first to win the European Cup three times. Inevitably, there were those who say this success made it worse for Shanks and there's perhaps some truth in that. Shanks wouldn't have been human if he hadn't felt the odd pang. Cruelly denied a shot at the ultimate prize in the San Siro, he had to watch his former No.2 feast upon it. Three times in seven years. And even when Shanks was invited to attend Paisley's third final in Paris, he still felt the cold shoulder – he was put up in a different hotel to the team.

The ultimate test of a dynasty is if it blinks when its creator has gone. But it's seldom seen like that. Seamless successions are rare too and have eluded leaders from Roman emperors to American presidents and Russian tzars. But Shanks can justly claim to have laid such solid foundations that his shy, reluctant heir was able to take Liverpool to even greater heights. Even if it was painful for him to watch.

It wasn't all grim for Shankly, though. He did spend more time with his family, which was, after all, the main reason he gave for his retirement. He had grandchildren now too and was able to help install his daughters in what he called 'nice homes'. And the fire still burned. None other than Ian St John wrapped up his own life story with a poignant reference to the man who had done so much to shape it. Wrote the Saint: 'I celebrate my wife and family and all the good men, in and out of football, who have enhanced my days. Even now, I cannot take my leave without one last image of the man who stood so high among them all. Not long before he died, and long after he had detached himself from his Anfield fortress, he visited my football school when I was taking a session with Ronnie Yeats. We were working on penalty kicks. Shankly loved nothing more than taking a penalty. A nine-year-old was keeping goal.

Shankly tore in and blasted home his kick. If the ball had hit the boy on the head it might have decapitated him. Shankly glowed and told the boy, "Don't worry son, Ray Clemence wouldn't have stopped that." By then Bill Shankly was an old and rather saddened man but something inside him still blazed.'

Other clubs began to feel the warmth. He was called upon for advice by many people in the game and not just his former players. There was only one offer of substance – to become general manager of Derby County – but it was their great rivals Nottingham Forest to whom he would unwittingly give the most assistance. Shanks had always been an admirer of Brian Clough. He wanted to sign him as a player and then noted what a brilliant manager he had become, leading Derby to the title in 1972. The admiration was mutual and when Clough, now at Forest, won promotion to the old First Division in 1978, he called upon Shanks for a bit of help.

Forest's first game back in the top flight was a tough-looking one at Everton. But the revamped visitors thrashed the Toffees 4-0. Perhaps anticipating a heavy defeat, Clough had arranged for Shanks to come into the dressing room afterwards. If he had wanted him to give them a lift, it was now about keeping their feet on the ground. Garry Birtles tells the story in Daniel Taylor's lovingly compiled *I Believe in Miracles*. 'That dressing room was usually sacrosanct,' Birtles begins. 'Clough wouldn't even let in the chairman, but when he swung open the door his face changed. "Come in," he said, "delighted to see you." We couldn't see who it was at first, but he said it like it must be the pope or the prime minister. "Bill, I'm just giving them a rollicking, telling them how poor they were, but I think you should do it." And it was Bill Shankly, the former Liverpool manager. Clough sat down with the rest of us and suddenly it was Shankly, this legend of the game, giving the team-talk for the next 15 minutes, with his hands in his pockets, in the classic gunslinger pose.'

How much that 15 minutes contributed to Forest's 'miracle' we'll never know, but just as Shanks had with Puskás's Magyars while at Workington, we have to assume that 'the magic rubbed off'. He told them not to get carried away as there was a long way to go. But he added that if they could play that well and Clough was manager: 'You can win it. Don't just be *in* the First Division, go and win it. Keep playing like that and you can win the championship.' They did.

By winning it, Forest were in the European Cup the following season as were Liverpool who had retained the trophy. Few felt Forest would even get to show their passports when the two English representatives were drawn to meet in the first round. But in the first leg at the City Ground, Nottingham, Forest showed they belonged in this company. Outplaying the defending champions, they won 2-0. Dalglish admitted: 'They made us look like novices.' Still, Liverpool weren't unduly worried about overturning the deficit at Anfield. Forest, though, might have been and this is where Cloughie pulled another masterstroke.

To counter any pre-match nerves before facing a raucous Kop on a big European night, he invited a guest to talk to the team on the bus to the ground. Birtles, a rookie who had opened the scoring in the first leg, remembers feeling 'incredibly nervous', yet being calmed by the presence of none other than ... Shankly. 'Don't ask me how that came about,' he says. 'It didn't seem normal, but not much ever did under Brian Clough. Shankly must have come to our hotel or something, and we took him to the game. I never asked why. You just didn't.'

Forest kept their nerve and a clean sheet, knocked Liverpool out and went on to win the trophy. Then they retained it, and Clough and his sidekick Peter Taylor were justly lauded for their incredible success. But for Shankly those two brief interventions, years after throwing in the towel, showed that he could still have a galvanising effect on players. Not Liverpool players – but their rivals. And for a brief spell at the end of the 70s, Cloughie's men had Liverpool's number.

For Shanks, instead of recharging his batteries, retirement had the opposite effect. As many suspected he would be, he was lost without the game. He really had lived for it, breathed it, slept it, ate it, gulped huge vats of it. And was never sated. Without training to take, teams to pick, players to spot and freezing late-night journeys home from one-horse towns, life lost much of its meaning.

Compared to the man who gave the 'Chairman Mao' speech, when the world seemed at his feet, manning a personal helpline for other managers was a heck of a comedown. He admitted that resigning was the biggest mistake of his life and now it couldn't be undone. For many he still had his aura, for others he became a tragic figure. But he was still a man of his word. Among his huge repertoire of quotes, death was a recurring theme. Besides the most famous one about its importance, there was the one about 'going to be the fittest man ever to die'. No one ever thought it, but he kept his word on that too.

In late September 1981, he suffered a heart attack and was taken to Liverpool's Broadgreen Hospital. At first, there was disbelief. As a fit 68-year-old non-smoker and virtual teetotaller, he seemed the last person to have heart trouble. He ran every day and looked a picture of health. He was Shanks, he was indestructible.

As the news sank in to a stunned city, hopes flickered that he would shrug it off. In their dreams, fans could almost picture him with the nurses on his release, saying that it was an outrageous hoax to hide a knee injury from his next five-a-side opponents. If only. There would be no more quips and no recovery; we would never hear the rasp of that 'Gatling gun' again. Three days later, he suffered another massive heart attack from which not even he could come back. He died the same morning. The shock was far greater than that felt on his retirement. Back then there was chatter, people questioning it; now the stunned, mournful silence was broken only by uncontrolled sobbing.

The whole of Merseyside and the game at large found it hard to believe he had gone. Or the way it had happened. Any premature death of a much-loved institution can seem like larceny and this one was a Category A exhibit. No one suspected he had anything less than a Rolls Royce engine in his chest anyway. So, when former Leeds adversary Johnny Giles said: 'He died of a broken heart', the contentious issue of his retirement was revisited. Keegan had said that Shanks's departure from the club was 'the saddest, saddest thing that ever happened at Liverpool'. It wasn't quite – the finality of death supersedes even the most devastating career shift. But as Shanks had been unable to find a meaningful follow-up, few thought the two events were unconnected. The club had to endure another round of criticism for their part in it but who knows? That they went on to scale even greater heights may have tipped him over the edge.

The final word has to go to his fellow Ayrshireman and legendary chronicler, McIlvanney, whose piece in *The Observer* on 4 October 1981 began: 'Opponents of Liverpool Football Club would be rash to assume that they have done with Bill Shankly. Once Bill's ashes have been scattered on the pitch at Anfield any visiting forward who is setting himself to score an important goal is liable to find suddenly that he has something in his eye. Certainly, Shanks would want us to believe in the possibility. Even after the results were in the papers, showing a scoreline against his men, he always refused to give defeat houseroom. Maybe we should follow his example and regard his death as just an ugly rumour.'

Chapter 13

*'I might get beat with a big word
or two but when it comes to getting
things to work it's different. I'm not
as soft a touch as people think ...'*

Bob Paisley

LIVERPOOL CARRIED on playing as if it *were* an ugly rumour. If the trophy wagon had come around more often after Shanks's retirement, it was on the timetable after his death. Six league titles in the next ten years and never out of the top two. Never had an English club revelled in such sustained dominance. And there was another European Cup too – a fourth. Only Real Madrid had more. All this without a 'proper manager'. Neither Shanks's retirement nor death had caused a blip.

Paisley, all chiselled Geordie vowels and as homespun as his beloved cardigan, was cannier than he looked. He told McIlvanney: 'I might get beat with a big word or two but when it comes to getting things to work it's different. I'm not as soft a touch as people think

…' He was neither an orator nor a motivator – at least not in his predecessor's mould. But, tactically, he just may have been Shanks's superior. And when it came to injuries, having taught himself physiotherapy, instead of shunning a player, according to George Scott, 'Paisley could put a cartilage back in and spot an injury before the player knew he had it.'

As the trophies rolled in, this unlikely recipient just kept things ticking over in his quiet, unfussy way. He ensured Liverpool continued to make brilliant signings, whether emerging or established stars. One or two took time to settle but, like Shanks, Paisley was patient, had faith in the recruitment process and didn't panic. This was a Second World War veteran who had helped defeat Rommel at El Alamein and relieve Tobruk. He also had a hand in the liberation of Italy; the first time he saw Rome, it was from inside a tank.

He and Shanks had learned that when it came to new recruits, it was best to cherry-pick two or three a year rather than make wholesale changes or none at all. This way there would be no complacency but no sense of upheaval either. The likes of Northampton's Phil Neal, Newcastle's Terry McDermott, Joey Jones from Wrexham and Ipswich's David Johnson suggested Liverpool were seeing something in them that others couldn't. Local youngsters, Phil Thompson, Jimmy Case and David 'Supersub' Fairclough were also breaking into the side. Geoff Twentyman's scouting network and Paisley's own beady eye surpassed themselves.

Two other ways he stuck to the Shankly template were in building from strength and with a Caledonian core. Shanks had once risked the wrath of his compatriots by claiming: 'If you've got three Scots in your team, you've got a chance of winning something. If you've got any more, you're in trouble.' In his side of the 60s, he confined himself to Yeats, Stevenson and St John as its cornerstones, and soon Paisley had a team built around Alan Hansen, Graeme Souness and Kenny Dalglish.

Dalglish came in for Keegan, who took The Beatles's trail to Hamburg once Old Big Ears had been won. The German club activated a £500,000 clause in his contract, which gave him a new challenge and a salary of £250,000 a year. At Liverpool, he was getting £12,000. As his departure drew closer, the word 'irreplaceable' was a common prefix for the Mighty Mouse. But Paisley had his replacement lined up and didn't blink at having to pay Celtic a British record £440,000 for him. Very soon 'King Kenny' was looking like an upgrade. Hansen came from Partick Thistle and Souness from Middlesbrough, and they took the European champions to another level. They were pretty good at drinking and banter too. They ran the show.

With Welshman Ian Rush, signed from Chester, eventually proving the perfect strike partner for Dalglish, Paisley achieved immortality within seven years. Later, in a rare acceptance speech for yet more accolades, even he couldn't resist a gloat. He quipped: 'I've been here during the bad times too. One year we were second.' Back then, the old joke about television viewers rang true: 'If you are watching in black and white, Liverpool are the team with the ball.'

What could go wrong? Empires are not meant to last for ever and history has shown that few see their demise coming. Liverpool's foundations seemed more solid than most. There was a huge fan base, the ground had been modernised, the team were unstoppable. Nope, as the 70s became the 80s and Liverpool got even better, what changed was the world and football's place in it. The economics of the game, to be precise.

Keegan's new salary was a glimpse of the future. Liverpool had just converted their main stand into an all-seater – thereby reducing Anfield's capacity to 45,000. Turnover in the 1978/79 season was £2.4m. Profit was just £71,000. John Smith told the *Liverpool Echo*: 'Whilst we are a successful football club, in economic terms, we are broke. Clubs like Liverpool cannot compete on money coming through the turnstiles alone.' As a business, it wasn't working. Profit had never been the prime motive – winning matches had. And Liverpool had won more than anyone. But even with a trophy room full to the brim, the bank account was empty.

Paisley's cup was running over but after yet another league and League Cup double he decided to bow out at the end of the 1982/83 season. Just 64, he wasn't much older than Shanks had been when he called it a day and Liverpool had again been expecting there was more to come. But this time there was no hesitation – Paisley had had enough. Often overlooked is that he had joined the club 20 years before Shanks and served it as a rugged left-half, captain, reserve-team coach and first-team trainer. In all it was 44 years but after he 'retired', first as advisor to Dalglish and then member of the board, he reached an unprecedented half-century.

But the absence of a succession plan was again highlighted. Paisley anointed his second-in-command Joe Fagan but what unfolded was an inaction replay of when Shanks retired. Paisley had grown into the job but had still felt more comfortable in a tank than behind a mic. Compared to Fagan, though, he was the Louisville Lip. Despite the constant grin behind the scenes, the genial Scouser showed an even greater reticence for the spotlight than Paisley. Publicly at least, in the Boot Room, laces were undone but tongues were tied. Eventually he was talked into it and, in another case of history repeating, he won the European Cup – in his first season of 1983/84. The Reds won the league, too, for the 15th time, which was almost double the eight titles of next in line, Arsenal. No one could touch Liverpool but what would derail the club were matters that were neither football nor finance-related, and no one could see coming. They were the tragedies of Heysel and Hillsborough.

Six years in a row English clubs had won the European Cup. First Liverpool, then Forest twice, Villa once and Liverpool twice more. Shamefully, English fans – although not those of these clubs – also held the European hooligan crown. By the mid-80s, domestic league games had to be rigorously policed – barbarians were at the gates, the railway stations and laying waste to city centres. Abroad, the majority of fans who did behave were deemed guilty until they proved their innocence. And they rarely got the chance.

It was this febrile atmosphere that Liverpool fans encountered at the Heysel Stadium for the 1985 European Cup Final against Juventus. With a decaying arena not fit for purpose, and impotent cops, it was a tinderbox. But what cannot be ignored is that Liverpool fans started it by charging towards Juventus fans who fled in panic causing a wall to collapse on them. Thirty-nine died, hundreds were injured. When forced by UEFA to go ahead with the game for fear there would be more trouble if they didn't, Liverpool, whose hearts were simply not on the field, lost 1-0 to a Platini penalty. Fagan, deeply affected by the disaster, didn't want to continue and would remain haunted by it for the rest of his days. In a succession of sorts, the club handed the job to Dalglish, who was 34 and still playing. He would initially lean heavily on Paisley for support.

But even this couldn't disrupt the trophy wagon's delivery round, as in Dalglish's first full season Liverpool won the league and FA Cup Double. And though he would sack Twentyman, the masterly signings continued – John Barnes and Peter Beardsley arriving in 1987. Many observers felt the football the Reds played with those two in tandem was as good as anything Anfield had seen. Alas, they weren't able to test it on the European stage. UEFA, heaping all the blame for Heysel on Liverpool 'hooligans', hit English clubs with a blanket five-year ban from European competition. The Reds got an extra three, later reduced to one. English football was a pariah and would pay a high price for its loneliness. Even more painful, Liverpool were treated as a pariah in England too – at least by the media and the Thatcher government.

Dr Rogan Taylor, a lecturer in football studies at the University of Liverpool, said a complex set of feelings surrounded the disaster because people were ashamed to face up to the uncomfortable reality of hooliganism. 'The feeling in the city was one of desperate, desperate shame and depression,' he said. 'We had a controversial local government at the time, and everything was going to hell in a handcart. There were only two great cultural sources of excellence – music and football. We had the best football team in the world, and this was a stab in the heart for the city. It was a black, black day.'

But 15 April 1989 was even worse. It was Liverpool vs Forest again in another FA Cup semi-final at Hillsborough. When the same two met there the previous year, warnings that the ground wasn't fit to hold a full house went unheeded. The loss of 96 lives (all Liverpool supporters) affected the club and the whole city far more deeply than Heysel had. It scarred its very soul. The media, led by *The Sun*, which sank to unprecedented depths, laid the blame squarely on Liverpool fans. *The Sun* even concocted vile stories of fans looting the dead. It felt like a sadistic assault on football in general and on Liverpool in particular.

Liverpool won when the game was eventually played and went on to beat Everton, of all teams, in the final. But the shocking scenes in Sheffield and the incredible outpouring of grief took their toll on Dalglish. He had gone to funeral after funeral and been an absolute rock throughout, but the pressure told and the following season, between replays of a titanic fifth-round FA Cup tie with Everton, he quit. Once again, Liverpool played the Boot Room card with Ronnie Moran becoming caretaker until Souness came back from Rangers to take permanent charge. But where previously there had been a punctuation mark, now there was a tearing up of the page.

Contrary to popular myth, Souness didn't get rid of the Boot Room – the club did when the adjoining press room was enlarged – but he didn't rush to replace it. He wanted to do things his way and he was in too much of a hurry – neither his style nor his signings were what the club had been used to. And it wasn't just the team that was becoming unrecognisable. Like all other top-flight grounds, Anfield was going to have to become all-seater, including the fabled Kop. A year earlier, John Smith had finally given up as chairman after no less than 11 league titles and four European Cups in 17 years. He had ushered the club into the modern era and his successor Noel White was one of the founding architects of the Premier League. But White didn't last long and in 1991 David Moores, nephew of Sir John, took over.

Football was in a state of flux. Clubs were being floated on the stock exchange and mystery man Michael

Knighton tried to buy Manchester United for £10m. But when the deal began to look dodgy, United chairman Martin Edwards called it off, took Knighton's ideas and began selling the club's soul – bit by sponsored bit – to the highest bidder. Liverpool, still trying to cling to its 'People's Club' reputation, even hesitated over perimeter advertising. But they had been pioneers in shirt sponsorship with a £100,000 deal from Hitachi in 1979. They would win another trophy – the FA Cup – in 1992 but it couldn't mask what was happening off the field.

After Hitachi, Crown Paints and Candy, Liverpool ended up with Carlsberg, the Danish beer giants, for sponsors in 1992. And so began probably the most enduring support of a football club there has ever been. Although they relinquished their main sponsorship to Standard Chartered in 2010, Carlsberg continued as beer sponsors and celebrated their 25th anniversary in 2017. In a tumultuous period for the club, the brewers paid for Shanks's statue and even grew special red hops to the sounds of the Kop (!) for a unique red lager. If only the ownership had been as steadfast as the Long Cool Danes.

Meanwhile, thanks to struggles on the field, the pressure told on the manager too, and he needed heart surgery. But Souness's fatal mistake was to give an interview to the hated *Sun* as he recovered. Unfortunately for him, the story was delayed and came out on the Hillsborough anniversary. His ticker did get better but, on Merseyside at least, his reputation never has. When

Moores, who was a personal friend, reluctantly removed him in January 1994, it was the first time Liverpool had sacked a manager since 1956. Moores, a traditionalist, turned to ex-Boot Room graduate, Roy Evans, as his replacement.

At first it looked as if the club was rediscovering its soul. Evans had served 35 years at the club as player, coach and now manager and introduced local youngsters, Robbie Fowler and Steve McManaman. But along with David James and Jason McAteer, they epitomised a new, cockier breed of player and flattered to deceive. Dubbed the 'Spice Boys' as a play on a popular girls' group, they wore matching white suits at Wembley – and then lost the 1996 FA Cup Final to United. You felt even Shanks's man-management skills would have been tested.

The board's response was to bring in a renowned disciplinarian. Enter Gérard Houllier. He had the CV and the patter – besides managing France he had been at the Clairefontaine academy and had even taught French in Liverpool schools. He was meant to join as a coach but when Moran retired, it was decided he should help Evans, so they became joint-managers. It was wishful thinking that it could last; it didn't, and by November 1998, Evans, an old-school Liverpool loyalist, decided to sacrifice himself. He resigned and was driven from the ground in tears.

In sole charge, Houllier set about a Shanklyesque revamp of the club. Both the squad and Melwood got an overhaul but it was mainly a foreign influx of players with just Fowler, Owen and an emerging Steven Gerrard as homegrown. Liverpool launched the new millennium by winning a treble: the FA Cup, League Cup and UEFA Cup in 2001. For good measure, they added the Charity Shield and European Super Cup. Under their unlikely French master, the silverware was stacking up. The Kop, initially dubious, dared to dream again.

Chapter 14

'Perhaps one day we'll have a splash, When Littlewoods provide the cash.'

From 'The Mucky Kid' by Stan Kelly-Bootle

IN THE early 2000s, as untold riches cascaded into football's coffers, unknown men stalked its corridors of power and commandeered its boardrooms. And like the French Foreign Legion of old, a grateful game asked no questions. Cowboys or kosher, it was difficult to tell; some had the wealth of nations at their disposal, others just pretended they had. Liverpool's naïve chairman never stood a chance. David Moores, of the Littlewoods pools dynasty, could have done with eight score draws himself – every week. Although far from skint, he was a few divisions below the Forbes Super League of oligarchs and sheikhs. Nor was he a match for the snake oil salesmen. By 2007, he had already spent the best part of four years trying to sell. Winning the pools was a dream for millions but owning them was no longer enough to keep a club at the top of the game. Unimaginable though it would have been to Shanks and his peers, Littlewoods could no longer provide the cash.

The decision to seek what Moores called 'a fantasy investor' was taken in 2003. It was two seasons after the false dawn of what some called 'the Plastic Treble', but not long after Roman Abramovich's arrival had shifted football's tectonic plates. There was also the seminal decision to leave Anfield and build a new stadium in Stanley Park. At the time, the chairman quietly admitted he couldn't keep up, but it wasn't until years later – and after he had come under sustained flak for selling to the bad guys – that the fulsome explanation came. Even then the words had to be prised out of him. But once he did open up, this most private of men poured his heart out in a cathartic 3,000-word tome to *The Times*. Published on 26 May 2010, it was a succinct summary of how the game had changed. Here's a taste: "in the wake of Euro 96 with the influx of more and more overseas superstars on superstar wages, I was aware the game was changing beyond all recognition and deeply worried, too, about my ability to continue underwriting the financial side. I was from the ever-decreasing pool of old-school club owners, the locally based, locally wealthy supporter like Jack Walker who stuck his money in out of his passion for the club. Football clubs were beginning to be seen as a source of profit rather than a source of pride; they were as much financial institutions as they were sporting legacies. The Abramovich era was upon us, and I knew that I could never compete."

All this was in stark and deflated contrast to the euphoria of 2001 and 2005. In a rare excursion into the limelight, the publicity-shy chairman had been cajoled into joining the players for their open-top bus parade to celebrate the treble – and sampled the adulation from the top deck. Half a million lined the streets and the *Liverpool Echo* caught the mood with a 'Hip, Hip, Houllier' headline on its front page. Not since 1978, when Paisley's Reds had returned with their second European Cup in as many years, had the city seen anything like it.

Head still spinning from the acclaim of the red multitude, Moores declared he would do everything 'within my power to win things for them on a regular basis'. Even the bus was dubbed the Triple Decker, but everyone knew it wasn't the real McCoy. All three trophies were lower carat items to the Premier League and Champions League, and Lady Luck might have been running the line. Even the FA Cup was considered a steal in some quarters. A Stephane Henchoz handball in the final was seen by fishermen in Cardiff Bay but not by the referee. Given a couple of sniffs, Michael Owen had been Faginesque.

It all happened in Houllier's second year of sole charge and hopes were raised that the elusive title would soon be on its way. They had been waiting 11 years and it already seemed an eternity. Godot had already arrived and was on his third pint in the Sandon. Shanks would have been sad to see the demise of the Boot Room influence with the departure of Roy Evans,

Glenbuck, the birthplace of Bill Shankly. (Photo: Jeff Gilbert)

Shankly addresses his players while manager of Carlisle United, 10 January 1951. (Photo Mirrorpix)

Liverpool manager Bill Shankly (left) and his new team of backroom staff (left to right): Bob Paisley, assistant manager; Joe Fagan, first team trainer; Ron Moran, second team trainer; Reuben Bennett, special duties; and Tom Saunders, youth trainer; pictured at Melwood 8 July 1971. (Mirrorpix)

Shankly greets the massive crowd at St George's Plateau following Liverpool's loss to Arsenal in the 1971 FA Cup Final. (Getty Images)

Shankly salutes the fans at Anfield following his team's draw with Leicester City. (PA Images)

Leeds United manager Brian Clough applauds Shankly as they walk out for the 1974 Charity Shield on 10 August. Kevin Keegan and Billy Bremner were both sent off in the 1-1 draw, which was Shankly's last game in charge of Liverpool. (Getty Images)

Liverpool fans pay tribute to their much-loved former manager Bill Shankly at Anfield on 3 October 1981 prior to the 2-2 draw with Swansea City. Shankly had passed away on 29 September. (Getty Images)

A banner on the Kop acknowledges the 100th anniversary of Bill Shankly's birth prior to the Premier League game against Manchester United on 1 September 2013 (Getty Images)

American businessmen George Gillett (left) and Tom Hicks pose inside the players' tunnel after their takeover of Liverpool FC on 6 February 2007. Gillett and Hicks reached a deal, thought to be worth £470m, to buy the football club. (Getty Images)

Liverpool fans with protest banners in the stands relating to owners George Gillett and Tom Hicks. (PA Images)

Liverpool owner John W. Henry and wife Linda Pizzuti sit on the Anfield bench prior to the Premier League match against Huddersfield Town on 26 April 2019. (Getty Images)

Liverpool's players and Jurgen Klopp celebrate winning the 2019 Champions League Final at the Metropolitano Stadium in Madrid. (PA Images)

Jurgen Klopp and his team parade the European Champion Clubs' Cup in Liverpool on 2 June 2019, after beating Tottenham in the final. Goals from Mohamed Salah and Divock Origi earned the Reds their sixth European Cup, a first trophy in seven years for the club, and a first victory in seven finals for Klopp. (Getty Images)

Jurgen Klopp celebrates after Liverpool's win against AFC Bournemouth at Anfield on 7 March 2020. (Getty Images)

but the Frenchman was assembling a squad that looked capable of ending the drought. An erudite man, fluent in English, Houllier, helped by having worked in the city, seemed to 'get' Liverpool. Besides cup success, a third-place finish in the league meant the Champions League awaited them the following season. Fans thought they were on the cusp of a glorious new era. Houllier had spent a fair bit but most of his signings had gelled. Henchoz and Sami Hyypiä would become the best central defence pairing since Alan Hansen and Mark Lawrenson. Shanks would have approved of the value-for-money buys as well as the core of Scousers.

But after a lacklustre start to the league campaign Liverpool received a devastating blow in October. The manager was rushed to hospital after complaining of chest pains during a home game with Leeds. Fans feared the worst when they heard he was still being operated on when they were going to bed. The operation took 11 hours. It was an aortic dissection, but he pulled through. He missed half the season and Kirkby-born defensive star of the 70s, Phil Thompson, took the reins.

Houllier eventually returned for the run-in, to a rapturous reception. Soon after, just a point off the top of the Premier League and in the last eight of the Champions League, he tempted fate once more, declaring: 'We are ten games from greatness.' We didn't know it at the time, but it was Liverpool's zenith under the Frenchman and his own as a manager. Understandably, he had lost weight and didn't look quite his old self – but nor did the team. Liverpool could only limp into second place – seven points behind Arsenal – and bowed out of Europe to Bayer Leverkusen. That phrase would come to haunt him and the club. Greatness? They weren't even close.

In the summer, Moores backed the manager to the tune of £18m – an amount he called 'huge in those pre-Abramovich days'. But Houllier lost his touch in the transfer market too and, unlike the previous summer, bought duds – El Hadji Diouf, Bruno Cheyrou and Salif Diao the most notorious. Gerrard, who was Young Player of the Year in 2001/02, called it 'the biggest waste of £18m in Liverpool's history', and it convinced the chairman to sell up. Under Houllier, the white suits had gone but what Moores needed was a white knight.

He was also aware that Anfield, storied and intimidating though it was, lacked the capacity to sustain a 21st-century European giant. For all the promise of 2001, as well as a new team, Liverpool needed a new stadium, but no one on the board had pockets deep enough to fund either. So, as he would later write: 'The search for suitable custodians began in earnest …' In 2002, the club opted to shift to nearby Stanley Park and planning permission was given in 2004. Two years later, Liverpool City Council granted the club a 999-year lease on the proposed site. Given the starring role Anfield has played in the club's history, it was surprising that most fans were in favour. At least it was close by and more of them would be able to get in.

Moores was well aware that finding the right owners wouldn't be a cakewalk. He said: 'We worked long and hard for the right person or institution, we followed up every lead. We *wanted* that fantasy investor to come forward – the infinitely wealthy, Liverpool-loving individual or family with the wherewithal to transform our dreams into reality.' But only two serious candidates emerged, and neither was in the fantasy league. One was Steve Morgan, a local builder already on the board, the other Thaksin Shinawatra, the Prime Minister of Thailand. Neither had nearly enough cash but cynics wondered whether the coffers of an entire country, which Thaksin would soon be accused of raiding, might offer richer pickings than a housing estate.

With the board in 'no stone unturned' mode, Chief Executive Officer Rick Parry was dispatched to Bangkok. But as soon as he got off the plane, he knew he was a pawn in a domestic game of political chess – and beat a hasty retreat. Amnesty International and Human Rights Watch were already on Thaksin's trail. Kavi Chongkittavorn, a senior editor at *The Nation* newspaper, summed up the prime minister as: 'A combination of the corporate dominance of Berlusconi, Chavez's populist approach and the thuggery of Mugabe.'

Blind eyes might still have been turned at some clubs – as long as a world-class striker was brought in – but not on politically savvy Merseyside. Quite what Shanks would have made of it doesn't bear thinking about. Even worse in many eyes, Thaksin was a United fan. But none of this stopped Manchester City from accepting him – with nary a peep.

By 2005 Abramovich's cash had bought Chelsea the title, Jose Mourinho was in his early pomp and a diminished Houllier had departed. And Moores still had no takers. Liverpool had won the League Cup yet again in 2003 but it was no consolation for slipping further away from the Premier League title. In the Frenchman's place had come Rafa Benitez, a highly regarded Spaniard whose Valencia side had twice eclipsed Real Madrid and Barcelona to win La Liga. He then managed to eclipse the whole of Europe by winning the UEFA Cup.

Under him, Liverpool scraped through the Champions League qualifier and made surprisingly heavy weather of the group stage. It took one of Anfield's most memorable goals to get through. In the 86th minute of the sixth and last game against Olympiakos, Steven Gerrard's stunning half-volley sent the Kop into ecstasy and earned a place in the pantheon of great European nights. On such occasions, living in a two-up and two-down terrace in Knotty Ash seems worthwhile.

There was to be another game in the same decibel league when 'shushing Maureen' brought his high-flying Chelsea to Anfield for the semi-final. A 6-2 aggregate thrashing of Bayer Leverkusen and a resolute defiance of Juventus in Turin had further ramped up the anticipation levels. The Blues were favourites but after a gritty, goalless draw at Stamford Bridge in the first leg, Liverpool took an early lead. It was the infamous 'ghost goal' from Luis Garcia that has haunted the Portuguese manager ever since. The Reds held out and the din wouldn't have eased his torment – it certainly could have woken the dead. Whether Garcia's effort crossed the line or not, Liverpool crossed an important Rubicon – they had reached their first Champions League Final and their 'European Cup Final' since Heysel in 1985.

But in Istanbul they were soon up against it. Outclassed and overrun by a rampant AC Milan, they were lucky to be only 3-0 down at half-time. So bleak was the outlook that some fans left the stadium. In certain time zones, some went to bed. But Rafa's measured team talk and the introduction of Didi Hamann turned the tide. The Italians had been celebrating but it was far from over. Those that stayed the course duly witnessed the Miracle of Istanbul. But up in the directors' box, David Moores still needed another.

The comeback would have unexpected consequences. It convinced Stevie G, who had admitted considering an offer from Mourinho, to stay with Liverpool. 'How can I leave now?' the breathless skipper gasped to the shell-shocked world. Clutching Old Big Ears, he didn't wait for an answer.

Among the gobsmacked Reds supporters on the Bosporus that night was a certain Sameer Al Ansari, a long-time fan who had scrounged a ticket off Parry. The Reds CEO would later tell the *Anfield Wrap*: 'One of my very good friends was going to come to the Champions League Final in 2005, but couldn't get his son out of school and asked "would it be okay to give my ticket to the guy who runs DIC [Dubai International Capital]?"

I said absolutely, he sounds like just the fella we ought to be meeting. I made contact with him in Istanbul.'

Al Ansari was smitten by what he had seen – more smitten than most. Within two weeks, Dubai International Capital, of which he was CEO, asked to see the books. The head honcho was Sheikh Mohammed bin Rashid Al Maktoum, the absolute ruler of Dubai. Although better known by the patrons of Aintree than Anfield, he was a well-established presence in the Forbes Fat Cat Super League. Moores thought he had found his 'fantasy investor'.

Chapter 15

'I'm handing it over to safe hands.
This is not someone coming over just
to make a quick buck. They are in it
for the long term.'

David Moores on selling to Hicks and Gillett

SUGAR DADDIES don't grow on trees. No more
the local butcher, baker, candlestick maker; these days
they come from unlikely corners – Hong Kong, India,
Florida, Malaysia. And have made their piles from
unlikely sources: hair dressing (or so it was claimed),
chickens, leverage buyouts, budget airlines. But mostly
they come from places where trees have long gone,
from deserts, hot and cold, where profits from the gunk
underneath keep them in well-appointed clover. David
Moores knew that on any prospective list of fantasy
investors, oil sheikhs and oligarchs would occupy the
Champions League positions. The trick was to find one
with a paternal instinct for a football club. So, it was to
Dubai, once an unloved British Protectorate but now the

New York of the Gulf, where he turned after discerning the first serious sniff. The CEO was an avid supporter and had the Liverpool badge as his screen saver, but what of the Mr Big?

Sheikh Mohammed bin Rashid Al Maktoum is the emirate's absolute ruler and the force behind its emergence as a global player. A renowned moderniser (of sorts), philanthropist, humanitarian, poet and patron of the arts, he has still found time to sire 23 children from six wives. What might be called his other breeding ground involves thoroughbred race horses; his Darley stud is the world's largest and his Godolphin stables have produced serial winners from the Preakness to the Prix de l'Arc de Triomphe. Not just a man of the turf but the royal highness of the sport of kings. What Moores wanted to know was: could this sheikh among sheikhs become His Royal Scouseness in his spare time?

Summer came and went. So did autumn. A new season was well under way, but he couldn't get an answer. Contact was no more than occasional. The perception on Merseyside was that the Arabs had gone cold on the deal. Maybe they didn't like what they saw. For this wasn't just a bog-standard takeover, it was about the rejuvenation of a giant – as well as building a new stadium. With a pot for Rafa Benitez to buy players, Liverpool were asking for just shy of half a billion quid.

As time dragged and Benitez pleaded for funds, Moores and Parry wondered what on earth the Arabs were playing at. They knew big deals didn't have to take long. Abramovich had agreed to buy Chelsea in ten minutes. And they knew the sheikh could have done likewise over a cup of karak chai if he had been inclined. After all, Dubai isn't a place where they get left in the stalls. Parry noted: 'Every time you'd visit Dubai it had changed, they'd built half a city, so you think these are the kind of people that get things done.'

On the field, the Reds had sent Al Ansari a few reminders. In August 2005 they won the European Super Cup, in December they were finalists in the World Club Cup and the following May they finished third in the Premier League. The standout was a memorable FA Cup win in 'the Gerrard final' of 2006. But it wasn't until August – 15 months after Istanbul – that DIC confirmed they were ready to do business.

Knowing that dilly-dallying wasn't in their prospective buyers' DNA had only amplified Liverpool's frustration – and they had already felt plenty. The football club might have been the 'Mucky Kid' to the equine aristocrats of the Middle East, but it was fed up with being mucked about. 'We had quite a few false starts with people claiming they could introduce us to senior sheikhs, and it turned out they couldn't. [It was just] mythical interest,' Parry recalled. 'It wasn't that uncommon to go for two days and come back not having met anyone at all.'

Moores had waited long enough to sell the family silver. He had made that decision with a heavy heart and now, adding to his burden, was the urgent need for funds for both team and new ground. He had to dip into his own pocket to buy Dirk Kuyt and steel for the stadium.

By now, though, not all Liverpool's eggs were in the Dubai basket. After the rebuff he had received from Doug Ellis when trying to buy Aston Villa, American businessman George Gillett returned to haunt the Premier League. Rejected because he had to borrow the cash – Ellis preferring another American, Randy Lerner, who had it – Gillett had joined forces with Tom Hicks. Already the owner of the Montreal Canadiens, Gillett was working up an appetite for a slice of the ever tastier Premier League pie. And in Hicks, who owned the Dallas Stars and Texas Rangers, he thought he had found the ideal partner. Besides their ice hockey and baseball portfolios, both men, already in their 60s, claimed to be active sportsmen – Gillett skied, while Hicks played golf and shot pheasant. As Brian Reade put it in *Epic Swindle*, 'Put them together and you've got James Bond. Look at them separately and you've got Tom and Jerry.'

Either way, the two Yankees were never going to be called Doodle and Dandy. Once Gillett had scented a kill, he wouldn't take no for an answer. And although Parry told him that Liverpool were going with DIC, he invited the CEO and Moores to Montreal. He laid on his private jet and let them talk to anyone who gave a puck about their team. It was November 2006, and he was manoeuvring into position in case anything went wrong with the preferred deal, a deal that wouldn't be preferred for much longer.

Moores and Parry were impressed. Besides being given the gushing official line from employees, they did their due diligence among fans and heard only good things about the owner. But the *pièce de résistance* was Gillett tearfully revealing that he had once gone bankrupt. Like the *mea culpa* of some evangelist preacher who had been whoring with the collection money, he won the Liverpudlians over – but not enough for them to do business. Liverpool-born Malaysia-based sports commentator Dez Corkhill says: 'They wouldn't have been swayed by that treatment. Categorically not. Moores was a wealthy man with working-class values. He wouldn't have been wooed by the jet.' Even after the virtuoso performance by Gillett, Moores still favoured what he thought would be the sovereign fund of an oil-rich state. No guarantees but national pride, he reasoned, would keep it on the straight and narrow.

Thinking it might expedite matters, Parry decided to tell DIC about Gillett and Hicks. And he offered to go to the Gulf with Moores and sort it out with Al Maktoum once and for all. Unlike Gillett, the hosts didn't lay on a private jet, nor loyal jockeys and stable boys to sing their masters' praises. But far worse than that, there was no Mr Big to talk to. The meeting with Al Maktoum was set for the next morning but the sheikh never showed up – he went for a gallop instead.

Short of tannoying it from the mosques with the call to prayer, Al Maktoum couldn't have announced his priorities more emphatically. Moores and Parry returned home in high dudgeon, doubts resurfacing about the suitability of the buyers. But business was still business. As Corkhill says: 'They would have been pissed off by the rudeness but it wouldn't put them off the deal. They still felt they were right for the club.' Indeed, they did. When DIC eventually came back to them with an offer of £450m on 4 December, Al Ansari's hand was nearly bitten off. He was invited over and given the royal Anfield treatment; he didn't just meet the board but Benitez and Gerrard too. After the glad-handing, DIC were granted exclusivity until mid-January.

Parry and Moores talked of securing the club's future for the next 100 years but the euphoria didn't last. Before the year was out, the *Daily Telegraph* ran a headline that suggested a very different lifespan: 'Buyers plan to sell Liverpool in seven years.' No burning blimp has ever deflated faster than the hopes of the two men who had devoted almost every waking moment of their recent lives to securing the future of Liverpool FC. The DIC plan, as outlined in a document seen by *The Telegraph*'s Mihir Bose, was to borrow £300m for what they saw as 'purely a business deal built around the new stadium' – and there would be no money for new players.

'Seven years, borrowed money and none for new players!' The two repeated the unpalatable bones of the deal to each other like a mantra as they huffed and puffed, the chairman like a chimney. So much for the sovereign fund, so much for the Abramovich of the Gulf – they didn't have the cash! It seemed scarcely credible but Moores believed the story to be authentic. It was. In summing up, Bose had written: 'The document also provides a wonderful insight into DIC's thinking but is very different from the fans' expectations of this purchase – and would have been very different from the purchase of the club by Gillett.'

'That's it, kick 'em out,' raged Moores. The board agreed. But by mid-January the chairman had calmed down. It was sufficient for Parry to pretend the deal was still on. Moores had shaken hands with DIC and believed in the sanctity of a gentleman's agreement. Not for the first time, he dithered. The other board members were telling him to forget the handshake. He did, but only when the exclusivity period was over.

Gillett had been hovering like a vulture. And once the deadline for DIC had passed, he swooped. He and Hicks swept through the Shankly Gates and in less than an hour, Liverpool FC was as good as theirs. They reassured the beleaguered chairman about his two principal concerns: that there would be no debt on the club, and the stadium would be built in time for the 2009/10 season. With Rothschilds ratifying the American duo's wealth, the board opted to kick DIC into touch. But Moores, still not comfortable with letting go the love of his life, asked for another 48 hours to think about it. He didn't get them.

When he phoned Al Ansari the next morning to tell him the board wanted to go in an alternative direction, the response was: 'If you don't commit to DIC by 5pm today, we're walking away.' According to Parry, Moores then said: '"You're not going to blackmail Liverpool Football Club. No one's going to treat us like that – we'll call your bluff." That was the final push that took the chairman in the other direction. An hour before their self-imposed deadline, DIC pulled out.'

An easy analogy to make – and many did – was of a bride changing her mind at the altar. The shocked congregation didn't know it, but it really had been something the Arabs had said – their insistence on a pre-nup when Liverpool thought it was till death us do part. But the courtship had never suggested it was love at first sight. They hardly saw each other, yet Moores believed DIC was 'the one'. He had already been trying to build their new home. But now, he turned to Gillett, who had never really gone away, and his new partner, Hicks. Another easy analogy: he was on the rebound and desperate not to be left on the shelf.

Just what Shanks would have made of these shenanigans doesn't bear thinking about. Perhaps it's best that he never had to endure them. Insiders said that Moores would change his mind according to how Liverpool were faring on the field. If they won, he wanted to keep them; if they lost, he was more willing to sell. Al Ansari wasn't to know, but in Istanbul he may have missed out on a bargain when they were 3-0 down at half-time.

But the flak they got was nothing compared with what was to come. Moores was accused of preferring the Americans because he made an extra £8m out of the deal. On that matter he maintained a dignified silence for many years but finally broke it in his *Times* letter. He flatly refuted the accusation that they didn't do 'even a Google search on Hicks and Gillett' before adding: 'And as for the extra money I netted from the G&H deal – you really don't know me if you think that was a factor.'

Sympathy was scant but Moores gets plenty from Corkhill. 'Liverpool have no bigger fan than David Moores,' he said. 'Yes, he did make a lot of money in the end but he did not sell to make money; he decided to sell because he realised he could no longer compete. Abramovich's arrival was the turning point. Everything he did was for Liverpool FC – Rick Parry coming in, Gérard Houllier coming in. Trying Roy Evans to keep a local heart to it. He tried everything. He was massively hard done by.'

On 2 February 2007, Gillett and Hicks offered £435m for the ownership of Liverpool. This included £215m for the building of a proposed new stadium on Stanley Park. The club's board, led by Moores and Parry, unanimously recommended that this offer be accepted. Four days later, it was, valuing the club at £218.9m (£5,000 per share), and confirming debts of £44.8m. In their original press conference, Gillett promised work on Liverpool's new stadium would begin immediately, saying: 'The spade has to be in the ground within 60 days.'

Chapter 16

'When I was in the leverage buyout business, we bought Weetabix and we leveraged it up to make our return. You could say that anyone eating Weetabix was paying for our purchase of Weetabix. It was just business. It is the same for Liverpool.'

Tom Hicks

JAMES BOND or Tom and Jerry? Whichever way you looked at Liverpool's new owners, they were an odd couple. Big Tom and Little George. Brash, bullying Texan and wily charmer from Wisconsin. Hicks was half a head taller and several zillion bucks richer than Gillett, who could be almost likeable. Albeit smooth-likeable, not-to-be-trusted likeable. If they were cops, they would be the bad and the not-so-bad; Tom would do the beating, George would do the handcuffs – with a smile.

Jonathan Northcroft, now the *Sunday Times* football correspondent, was on that beat at the time and met them. He says: 'Gillett [was] very charming but slippery. Hicks was basically cut from the same cloth as JR and George W. Bush. Their mistake was thinking the UK was like the US in terms of the power being in charge of a business buys you. They were shocked when the bank and lawyers wrested control of LFC from them. Hicks was always painted as the bad guy but for me the bigger villain was Gillett – a huckster with no actual money of his own to put in.' He'd had money but lost it.

Doug Ellis had seen Gillett coming from 5,000 miles away, but Liverpool 'had got to know him', as Parry put it. Or thought they had. Cunning to his hiking bootstraps – he wore comfort shoes after wrecking his knees on the ski slopes – he charmed Moores's wife Marjorie once he had sensed that she wore the trousers. He called himself an investment banker but that hadn't stopped him going bust. Now he was on the comeback trail and had a big guy in tow.

He and Hicks had little in common apart from their wives' love for art, siring 'soccer-loving' sons and each owning an ice rink. Nowhere near enough to make them soulmates. But when it came to using other people's money to cut a deal, make a huge profit and run, they were as thick as ... well, leverage buyout merchants.

But when it came to a fit, they didn't. Not with each other and certainly not with Liverpool. As Paul Hayward, then of *The Guardian*, memorably put it: 'A club synonymous with the earthy virtues of Shankly,

145

Paisley and Dalglish rebuffed a suitor wealthier than Roman Abramovich to foxtrot with George Gillett and a partner who showed up later than a mystery man in a Hollywood thriller.' Hicks is from Dallas and best buddy of the 43rd President. He's also a neighbour – their ranches are in the same hemisphere. Those earthy virtues were disappearing over the Texan horizon.

In the 'Greed is Good' 80s, Hicks had donned his ten-gallon Stetson and filled that and his cowboy boots. He amassed a middle-ranking fortune and was known as the man who made George W. Bush rich. But when it came to sport, his Midas touch deserted him. In 2000, he made what the US papers called 'the worst deal in baseball history' by buying superstar Alex 'A-Rod' Rodriguez for the Texas Rangers on a ten-year, $250m contract. It would make Liverpool's signing of Andy Carroll look a canny piece of business.

Asked what he made of the Yanks' presentation, SOS's Mike Nevin said: 'Very American, very jarring.' Reade compared it to 'a Seventh Day Adventist Bible-Sellers' convention. What particularly grated were the fixed smiles, red ties and pinstripes of their sons. He had 'half-expected Michael Knighton's ball-juggling act at Old Trafford' of a generation ago. Like Knighton and Ali Baba, they felt they had stumbled upon the treasure that no one else could see. Hicks would say: 'The more I looked, the more I became convinced it was an opportunity to buy a crown jewel of sports at a modest price.' To twist an old quote, the deal would have much for them to be modest about.

CHAPTER 16

The two guarantees the Liverpool owner demanded
of the American duo were that they would build the
stadium and not do 'a Glazer'. He said that when he
asked for assurances, he had looked them in the eye.
They didn't blink. Hard-nosed, hard-eyed. Gillett also
had to vouch for Hicks. Moores admitted to *The Times*,
'to a great extent we took Tom on trust.' Whether it
was Rothschilds examining the books or the chairman
peering into their retinas, they passed muster.

Gillett was a man who made his own luck and rode
with it. His big break came when NFL Commissioner
Pete Rozelle, overlooking the missing 'e' at the end of
his name, mistook him for a clean-shaven heir to the
toiletries empire. He gave him a lead into the Miami
Dolphins. Even so, his business career mirrored his
efforts on the ski slopes. He would have falls but always
got up. Traipsing into a boardroom in boots gave him
a slightly comic appearance. There was a Napoleon
complex too; he was short in stature but loved the
big names. The Canadiens were the most storied in
ice hockey. He also bought the Harlem Globetrotters.
Liverpool made for a heady threesome.

As the *Anfield Wrap*'s Gareth Roberts admits, back
in early 2007: 'It did seem rosy. I remember when they
first came, there were banners on the Kop and people
did see them sort of like saviours. They were going to
take Liverpool up to another level, that old phrase. It
was pitched that they were the ones who would build
the stadium. It was how it was presented and you're a
fan and you want to believe.'

Moores had set as much store in getting the stadium built as keeping the club debt-free. Anfield's capacity was now cut to a mere 42,000; Liverpool were squeezed more than most clubs with the shift to all-seater stadiums. But that's what comes of standing room where there's only a back pocket to piss in. The Kop was going to be the biggest loss, but times – and attitudes – change; no one ever saw seats being on it till Hillsborough. But everyone wondered whether a new Kop could ever be the same.

It had been the club's 'extra man' since 1906. Originally called the Oakfield Road Embankment, it was made of ash and cinders and formally renamed the Spion Kop after a hill in Natal, South Africa. The name 'Kop' was also in homage. It was the site of the Battle of Spion Kop in the Second Boer War, where over 300 Lancashire Fusiliers died. Many were from Liverpool and no less a figure than Mahatma Gandhi carried them down – he was a stretcher bearer for the British Army.

Working as a lawyer in South Africa at the time, he formed the Natal Ambulance Corps, and in 1900 volunteered for duty on behalf of the British Empire. Also on that original Kop was none other than Winston Churchill. And so, on the same hill, on the same day, on the same side were two of the 20th century's greatest political antagonists. Midway through the century, they would joust over Indian independence from Britain in one of history's heavyweight contests: the father of the emerging nation against the great imperialist. Churchill would later concede: 'It may have been better had we met.' They almost did. Writes Arthur Herman in *Gandhi & Churchill*: 'They must have passed literally within yards of each other, since one of the men Gandhi carried was the mortally wounded General Woodgate.' Churchill witnessed the scene as a reporter for the *Morning Post* but never thought to get a quote from a stretcher bearer. Gandhi was awarded the Queen's South Africa Medal for his bravery and dedication to duty. It was one of history's great 'ships in the night' moments.

Sixty days passed and the only spades that went into Stanley Park belonged to the local parks department. None were from LFC. The deadline was missed but somehow – it was still the honeymoon period – it went largely unnoticed. The team were heading towards another Champions League final and the owners were redrawing the plans – for an even bigger stadium.

They now had the seal of approval from the skipper, although his deputy harboured doubts. Gerrard said: 'They made promises and were very convincing. To hear from their mouths about their plans to improve the stadium and build a new team was at the time brilliant. Obviously, it would be a wrench to leave Anfield, but I thought it would be amazing to lead Liverpool out in a new stadium as captain.' Jamie Carragher wasn't so sold on the owners. He said: 'In the back of my mind I was thinking "this isn't right". One of them hasn't got the cash and the other really doesn't want to be here; this could end up going wrong. Also, I wasn't happy with joint bosses. We should have known better after having Roy Evans and Gérard Houllier as joint managers. I don't care what anyone says, there has to be a number one in everything. Eventually there's going to be a problem and they'll end up falling out.' He didn't know how prescient those words would be.

The first seeds of doubt in Carra's mind had been sown by Rio Ferdinand. The whisper from Manchester was that the Glazers were dreading a DIC takeover. He was told they feared 'another Abramovich', whereas they knew about Hicks and Gillett, and were desperately hoping their fellow Americans would get it. It made Carra wonder: 'Hang on, have we made a mistake here?'

Paul Tomkins, the man behind the *Tomkins Times*, also got wind of criticism but admits: 'They seemed alright at first but a friend in the States kept e-mailing me and saying, "These guys [Hicks & Gillett] are not good owners – they have a really bad reputation." He called them cowboys.' Corkhill was also initially taken in. He says: 'The first things they did were great. Liverpool suddenly went out and bought [Fernando] Torres and other great players. Benitez was able to concentrate on his team for a year or so, and it looked great. We were in the Champions League final again with a massively over-achieving team.'

In March 2007, a *Guardian* exposé by David Conn suggested they had 'done a Glazer' after all by borrowing just shy of £300m and loading the debt on to the club. The story appeared just five weeks after the takeover, yet hardly any fuss was made. Brian Reade wondered:

'Was it because it was in *The Guardian* or maybe that people just didn't want to believe it was true?'

Under the new owners, form had picked up after an indifferent start to the season and, from the reaction of the fans, it seemed the Americans were getting much of the credit. As Moores recalls in his letter, 'George and Tom were carried shoulder high through the city centre on the afternoon of the Barcelona game in March 2000.' Benitez had masterminded a famous victory over the Catalans with Craig Bellamy and John Arne Riise scoring in the Camp Nou. They would lose the home leg 1-0 but went through on away goals. Riise might also have 'lost a leg' when Bellamy whacked it with a golf club. Another distraction. Anyway, why let a bank loan get in the way of knocking out Barcelona?

After PSV Eindhoven had been outclassed in the quarter-final, the hated Chelsea turned up at Anfield once again. The Blues were in contention for the quadruple, which ensured another feisty occasion. Predictably the Londoners were met by a wall of sound as they had been just two years earlier. Hicks and Gillett were taken aback. After another titanic contest, Liverpool prevailed on penalties to reach their second final in three years. They were at the pinnacle of world club football again and, three months in, the owners were still onside.

The final was not just a disappointment, more the climax of a week-long debacle. If Istanbul was a miracle, Athens was an overdose of harsh reality. AC Milan gained revenge for their 2005 collapse with a 2-1 win.

Liverpool hadn't performed and many fans – the lucky ones – hadn't been allowed in. Parry copped the blame for that, but Hicks and Gillett were no longer to be trusted. The cat was out of the bag, but it took a second story before it sank in.

On the eve of the match, Hicks had admitted they were using club profits to pay interest on their loan. And in trying to pass it off as normal practice, he dug himself into a deeper hole. He said: 'When I was in the leverage buyout business, we bought Weetabix and we leveraged it up to make our return. You could say that anyone eating Weetabix was paying for our purchase of Weetabix. It was just business. It is the same for Liverpool: revenues come in from whatever source and go out to whatever source and, if there's money left, it is profit.'

What is best remembered from this disastrous Greek odyssey is the way the club's most loyal fans had been left to feel they didn't matter. Of many sins committed that week, for them this was cardinal. And what Shanks would have made of it, we hardly need to ask. For the first time in Liverpool's then 115-year history, fans staged a protest march against their own club. Meanwhile for Moores, his heart didn't just sink, it was around his ankles. When Hicks and Gillett bought the club, they borrowed the money rather than dip into their own personal fortunes.

Other cracks had been emerging in the star-spangled façade. Parry had never really got on with either of the owners; nor had Rafa. But even more troubling was that the owners weren't getting along with each other. They were said, by one official, to loathe each other. And Rafa, who might have been Niccolo Machiavelli in a previous life, wasn't busting his considerable gut to be peacemaker.

All he wanted was new players and all he was getting was flattery. Tired of banging on about signings, he had got the two owners to agree to a post-match meeting to thrash out the summer transfer policy once and for all. When they cancelled at the last minute because of their private jet departures, he let rip at everyone, including Parry. And this combined with the Champions League defeat, debt issue and 'the breakfast of champions' would ensure the honeymoon was over. Or so we thought.

Chapter 17

'If Rafa said he wanted to buy Snoogy Doogy, we'd back him.'

George Gillett

'BRITAIN AND America are two countries divided by a common language.' No one knows who had the copyright on that little gem, but Winston Churchill, George Bernard Shaw and Oscar Wilde are the leading candidates. It's a pithy line but, in normal discourse, the divisions are not that great; it's only in sport where it seems there might be two languages.

It certainly appeared that way with Hicks and Gillett. It wasn't just their manner that was 'very American, very jarring', it was their lingo. There are no play-offs in the Premier League, as officials tired of telling them. Liverpool have never beaten anyone 'two to one'. Nor had Stevie G ever scored from 'downtown'. Yet the irony was the first person this gobbledygook would drive to distraction was a Spaniard, Rafa Benitez.

If he had been given any players 'in the draft' it might have kept him quiet, but he was appalled by the crass behaviour, and being stood up in Athens was no surprise. What rankled was the lack of respect the Americans and their sons displayed for the Liverpool Way. When he had arrived from Valencia, Benitez and his wife Montse had immersed themselves in Shankly lore and soon passed as honours grads. He has since managed Inter, Real Madrid, Chelsea, Newcastle and Dalian, China, but the family home is still in the Wirral, his daughters have Scouse accents and if offered the job back, you get the feeling he would do it for a pittance – as long as he got the players he wanted.

Athens proved a tipping point. He spent the night pounding the wet streets because of overbooking – he let the wife of a coach share his room with Montse. But he was in no mood to put his head down anyway. His fury had barely abated when he delivered his tirade the next morning. The assembled hacks weren't prepared for his broadsides and were shocked that he targeted Parry as well as Hicks and Gillett. But Benitez, who, after 'asking for a table and being given a lampshade' at Valencia, strummed a familiar tune – he just switched from the front room to the garage. 'Here is the truth,' he claimed. 'I am driving an old BMW while Ferguson and Mourinho are driving Ferraris. I have to swerve and cheat to beat them, and I can do that, but I need the money and the back-up to beat Ferraris.'

The groans from across the Atlantic might have been heard on the Wirral given a strong westerly, but

Hicks and Gillett, although inwardly seething, had little choice but to cough up. Or, rather, get the club – via the all-too-willing banks – to add to its debt. Benitez was given £45m to spend, and with half of it he bought a 'Ferrari' of his own – a veritable Testarossa. Fernando Torres certainly had the acceleration, only one owner – his home town club Atlético de Madrid – and, just 23, was already a star for Spain. He also had a choirboy face that masked a killer instinct. Dubbed 'El Nino' (The Kid) in Spanish, many thought he was nicknamed after the weather phenomenon – especially as he took the Premier League by storm. It showed what Benitez could do with a bit of cash on a forecourt. The luxury SUV, Javier Mascherano, also came, initially on loan, along with a trio of Fiats, Yossi Benayoun, Lucas Leiva and Ryan Babel. But half the outlay was recouped with a departing motorcade of bangers that included Bellamy, Cisse, Garcia and Sinama-Pongolle.

The owners hadn't only concealed the debt, they disguised their feelings towards the manager. 'If Rafa said he wanted to buy Snoogy Doogy, we'd back him,' quipped Gillett. It would become one of their classics in a bulging lexicon. With Parry the convenient fall guy over the ticket allocation and all eyes on where the money was going and not where it came from, the owners dodged a hail of bullets. And when they followed the Torres signing with plans for a 'bigger and better' new stadium, their heads were back above the parapet. The loan business notwithstanding, in an *Echo* poll, 90 per cent of fans approved of the 'new Anfield'.

Hicks hadn't been happy with the previous design – it wasn't big or brash enough for his Texan tastes – so he hired Dallas architects HKS and demanded something more eye-popping. In doing so, he rode roughshod over the original plans, which could have been adapted to hold 70,000 at much less cost, as well as Gillett. The Wisconsin Kid had already detected the chill winds of recession blowing across America and wanted to draw down the expenses. It was an open secret now that he and Hicks were no longer seeing eye to eye.

Hicks was the alpha male to Gillett's obsequious beta. With more money, he was less concerned by the looming crisis than his partner and wanted to replicate the intimidating atmosphere of Anfield. One thing he did 'get' was the pre-eminence of the Kop and got his message across to HKS. When he saw the new drawings, he could hardly contain himself. 'It's spectacular and I can't wait for everybody to see it,' he said of the new 70,000-seater, £300m futuristic masterpiece of steel and glass. 'I think our fans will love it. It's very creative architecture, very contemporary but unique to Liverpool as it's all centred around the Kop.' He was right – the fans did love it and, all too briefly, we witnessed football's unique ability to bond polar opposites: staunch socialist fans and rabid capitalist owners were somehow still on the same page when it came to Liverpool FC.

Would Shanks have liked it? For him it would have been sacrilege to ever think of leaving Anfield, but he might just have approved of the new Kop. It was to be single tier but have a capacity for 18,000. And there would be no need for a sign to remind visitors where they were playing. Above all else, it was forbidding. If Darth Vader had a football team, it's where they would play. The ball would once again be terrified.

No sooner had these artist's impressions made eyes pop than Liverpool beat Derby 6-0 to go top of the league on 1 September. The new design was approved by the city council in November and the stadium was scheduled to open in August 2011. To outsiders, autumn of 2007 probably marked the zenith of the Hicks/Gillett reign, which had somehow recovered from Athens. On the field, the team was gelling, and Torres looked a worthy heir to the striker crown. Anywhere else, all this might have quelled the rumblings about where the cash was coming from – Liverpool had begun the season with their longest unbeaten run since 1991 – but peace steadfastly refused to break out.

The owners rarely came over but that didn't stop the manager from pestering them – by email, by phone and via Parry. The new signings weren't enough to pacify Benitez, who knew his side was far from complete. Hicks and Gillett became sick of it. In late 2007, with Liverpool riding high in the league under a manager who had led them to two Champions League finals in three years, they began to look for his replacement.

It was Gillett who led the search. He owned a ski resort in Vail, the Colorado town where world-renowned knee surgeon Richard Steadman had his clinic. It was a sensible precaution for an inveterate skier with dodgy knees. But it also enabled Gillett to ingratiate himself with famous footballers who had gone to get their cruciate ligaments fixed. It said much for his slimy traits that if his day job was running storied sporting franchises, he moonlighted as a groupie. He had even 'bumped into' Robbie Fowler on one occasion. Then he 'came across' Jürgen Klinsmann. 'An impressive man,' was Gillett's verdict on the German World Cup star.

Breaking their silence, he suggested to Hicks, who had never heard of Klinsmann, to do a Google search. There wasn't much he hadn't won as a player, but the clincher was that Klinsie lived in California where Hicks had a second home. The Texan duly invited the German and his American wife Debbie around for dinner. A convivial evening ended with Klinsmann being effectively offered Benitez's job. It was Thanksgiving 2007 – two days before Liverpool played Newcastle at St James' Park. With the time difference, just as they were on the port and cigars in the Golden State, Benitez was serving up unpalatable sound bites at his pre-match press conference on the Tyne.

Even before they had decided on Klinsmann, Hicks, in that Texan way of his, had told Benitez to shut up and concentrate on 'training and coaching' his team. The words wouldn't be forgotten. The Spaniard repeated the instruction mantra-like to the media before the Newcastle game. To the question, 'Do you know how much you will have to spend from the American owners in January?' he answered: 'I am focused on training and coaching my team.' To the question, 'Is there anything upsetting you?' he answered: 'I am focused on training and coaching my team.' To every question, his answer was the same. He repeated those words 25 times. Hicks and Gillett were at least in agreement on the manager, but both wondered who they should call first: Klinsmann or the men in white coats.

Gillett confided to journalists that he genuinely believed Benitez had mental problems and concocted a name for his condition – 'serial transactionist'. But as always with Señor Machiavelli, there was method in his apparent madness. He may have overdone the sarcasm, but it was his way of highlighting the difference between the general perception of his role and what it actually was. In his 2012 book *Champions League Dreams*, he revealed that he had been lumbered with extra duties. 'I was suddenly supposed to be a bank manager,' he wrote. The trouble was the bank had no money. Liverpool's form began to falter but not as badly as the world economy. The owners suddenly had a lot more to worry about than a disaffected manager. Gillett's fears of impending doom hadn't been unfounded.

Amid the rumours of a credit crunch in the US, the names Fannie Mae and Freddie Mac raised a few eyebrows. Some thought they might make up Gillett's fantasy midfield with Snoogy Doogy. But the mortgage lenders were leading players in the American financial crisis. The crash of 2008 was coming and, although fans didn't know it at the time, it would have profound implications for Liverpool FC. A squeeze to compulsive borrowers was like a tsunami to coastal fishermen. Not only would there be no money for Rafa, there would be none for the stadium.

The fans, like the wider public, may not have had the best vantage point for spotting the first fissures of financial meltdown. But when it came to the future of their much-loved manager, they had a finely tuned sixth sense. Long before WikiLeaks was a twinkle, the word on the street was that if Liverpool failed to beat Porto and thereby miss out on the Champions League knockout stage, Rafa would be sacked. It was four days after the win at Newcastle and banners were unfurled – some even in Spanish – and chants were chanted, all for Rafa to stay. It was so overwhelming that Benitez was moved to say: 'Where have you ever heard in your life, anywhere in football, this kind of support for a manager?'

In the event, Liverpool thrashed Porto 4-1 and Rafa stayed. They then scored four more past Bolton before surprisingly losing their unbeaten record to Reading. But that did nothing to stem the tidal wave of support for the manager. Hostile sounds on Merseyside, chill winds at home, the owners were discovering the harsh reality of running a football giant in a foreign land at a time their own nest eggs were being threatened. They didn't 'get' the club, they didn't 'get' the sport or the city and, when cornered, couldn't even agree on their escape route, their own shotgun marriage having split asunder. Gillett's cold feet were a legacy of his previous encounter with the bailiffs. In contrast, Hicks wanted to tough it out, and in the unlikely confines of the

Yorkshire moors, thought he may have found a saviour.

If millionaires do business on the golf course, billionaires make deals while shooting pheasant. Hicks, even with his endangered pile, was still just about in that league, while the glamorous Englishwoman he met on that autumn day in the north represented one of the world's richest men – none other than Sheikh Maktoum. Dubai had rekindled their interest in the club and the big man of the turf was coming up on the rails.

As one director noted: 'When Amanda Staveley is around, it's time to get the trebles in,' and Hicks's head was certainly turned. Still a mere princess of the game – it was before she helped secure Manchester City for Sheikh Mansour – Staveley was already a trusted advisor to the Middle Eastern elite, especially in Britain, but it was the mention of Maktoum that grabbed the Texan's attention. While Gillett was already trying to weasel out of Liverpool by selling his half of the club, Hicks was still hoping to make a killing.

For demanding supporters read demanding creditors. The owners reacted to the crisis as only leverage buyout merchants can – by heaping their entire acquisition debt on to Liverpool FC. It was legal as long as all board members gave written guarantees that, for the next year, they would repay all creditors. Moores and Parry were asked to sign. It was the final Champions League game at Marseilles and the pair were invited up to Gillett's suite. Scarcely believing what they were hearing, the Liverpool duo told the American in blazing terms what they thought of it, refused and stormed out. Hicks was absent but Moores now knew, without a shadow of a doubt, that he had sold the family silver to a pair of con men. He may have got personal assurances that there would be no debt loaded on the club but there was no legal guarantee. His worst nightmare had been realised.

The fixtures were coming thick and fast – next up was Manchester United at Anfield, but off the field they were just as tasty. The day after was a clear-the-air showdown between the owners and Parry and Benitez. The only surprise was the fumigators weren't called. But the manager cut straight through the fog – he looked both Hicks and Gillett in the eye and asked whether they had met Klinsmann. 'Yes, but only for consultancy work,' was their answer. Slippery as ever, they wriggled off the hook. Neither Benitez nor Moores would make it as opticians.

Gillett had the audacity to repeat the phrase at a Former Players Association Christmas dinner that night. 'Consultancy' can cover a multitude of sins and the owners were certainly committing them. They simply had no shame and Gillett was even applauded for saying, with a straight face, 'Benitez is the one we want as manager and we intend to keep him on.' But Hicks, when pressed by the *Liverpool Echo* after returning home, admitted Klinsmann had been their 'insurance' in case Rafa went to Real Madrid. The difference was significant – and pounced upon. After emailing the story to Hicks for him to approve, which to the paper's amazement he did, the *Echo* ran with it

under the headline: 'Hicks: We Lined Up Klinsmann.'
Fuses were lit all over Merseyside.

Chapter 18

'It's true to say that if Shankly had told us to invade Poland we'd be queuing up ten deep all the way from Anfield to the Pier Head.'

Post on Red and White Kop

AS SHRINES of protest go, the Sandon pub in Anfield ranks a safe distance behind the Berlin Wall and Tiananmen Square. It has been gentrified now but it will always hold a defiant significance in the history of Liverpool FC. Besides being where they broke free from Everton in 1892, it's the place fans said 'enough is enough' in January 2008. A bog-standard, working-class boozer back then, the Sandon was rammed with 300 hard-core Reds. What they had come to discuss was more than just the ownership – they wanted their voices heard on a raft of issues. And this time, there would be no scratching of quills in a cosy fug; the debate was deafening and the crowd spilled on to the streets. Long before the phrase became fashionable, they wanted their

165

club back. And as befits a predominantly socialist city, they formed a union.

Playwright Nicky Allt was the driving force. He had got together different branches of the Supporters Club and united them under the banner, Sons of Shankly. In a nod to real and political correctness – Shanks had two daughters – it was soon changed to Spirit of Shankly. But as long as the great man's name was in the title, everyone was happy. More than a quarter of a century after he had died, one Red and White Kop (RAWK) poster still felt moved enough to write: 'It's true to say that if Shankly had told us to invade Poland we'd be queuing up ten deep all the way from Anfield to the Pier Head.'

Another RAWK scribe spoke for many when he wrote this of Shankly: 'I really think that collectively we have not awoken from his spell. We still crave him and seek him out in our manager, and in the idealised relationship with the club and our leader that we all have in our minds. The affection and devotion that we show to Rafa is part of this. Our relationship with our boss is still shaped by the relationship we had with Shanks. We want our manager to be in his image. To inspire us and make us dream and have the same kind of swaggering wit and intelligence and messianic belief in us as a club, as fans, and as a city.'

He continued: 'We are known as a manager's club. It might even be a weakness sometimes. But more often than not, it's about wanting to see the club personified in a single figure that we can show immense devotion to. And that is all because of the magic weaved by Bill Shankly. We're still living in his afterglow and he has moulded the minds of all of us, even the Liverpool fans who weren't born when he retired. Like I said, we are still in his spell. Almost 40 years have passed and we are still mesmerised by him.'

What the great man would have made of Hicks and Gillett, we can only guess, but we can be pretty confident that it would have been as colourful as it was withering. Given what he did to Paddy Crerand, we could have been in for a treat. Think of Shankly's socialism, imagine the polar opposite and you wouldn't be far from the 'greed is good' credo of Gordon Gekko without the quips. Shanks would have cut through the owners' double-talk with one rasp of that Ayrshire tongue. He was no clairvoyant, but we feel he would have seen them coming before they even boarded their private jets on the other side of the Atlantic. Well, we like to think so anyway.

It wasn't even a year since the takeover and it had come to this. All the steely-eyed pledges, all the smarm, all the spade-in-the-ground bullshit ... Stanley Park was still unbroken but that wasn't the case with their promises. Snoogy Doogy had still not been signed, Rafa wasn't happy and nor were the fans. The team? Contenders but not champions. The master tactician took Liverpool deep into the Champions League with wins over Inter Milan and Arsenal before going down narrowly to Chelsea in the semi. In the Premier League they finished fourth but Torres's 24 goals broke Ruud van Nistelrooy's record for the most in a debut season. The Spaniard was top of the range but no one else was even in his slipstream – Rafa was still having to 'swerve and cheat'. For a club wracked by turmoil, reaching the last four of the biggest club competition in the world was no mean achievement. But it didn't stop the protests.

Corkhill believes that at this time even the manager lost his focus. 'Rafa had to take his eye off the ball to fight the political battle within the club,' he says. 'Look at his signings compared to the previous year.' Taking their cue from SOS perhaps, the *Echo* said: 'The American dream is for them over and beyond repair,' and called on Hicks and Gillett 'to do the decent thing'.

Just a few short months earlier, there hadn't even been a hint of a problem, let alone a crisis; but now it was full-blown and desperate. In the autumn, Torres had been scoring, the team had been winning and the stadium plans were approved. As that unmentionable Murdoch rag might have put it: 'It was the debt wot did it.' Even if news of it had taken a while to register. But when it did, there was no turning back. Already there were banners: 'DIC in – Yanks Out'. Divorce was the only option. By any standards – shotgun, Hollywood, convenience or mail order – this marriage hadn't taken long to hit the buffers. But even more than a decade later you still have to ask how it had come to this – and so quickly.

Hicks and Gillett had been shamed as fast-buck merchants, but no one could be more capitalist than DIC – a grasping forearm of the fabulously wealthy emirate set up for the whole purpose of making a swift buck for themselves. Their original intention to sell Liverpool after seven years – a ruthless acquisition and sale policy by any standards – had been rejected by David Moores. Hicks and Gillett hadn't gone for a gallop when Moores and Parry had turned up for a meeting. And at least they had seen a game or two – Sheikh Maktoum couldn't be bothered. So, why were Liverpool fans demonstrating with revolutionary zeal to swap one set of vulture capitalists for another?

A spokesman for Reclaim the Kop said: 'The fans want GG and TH out unconditionally. It's as simple as that. They are not good for us and no good for the club.' Liverpool fans felt they had been crossed and still harboured hopes that DIC would be their Abramovich. The news that they were back in the picture was enough to fuel their anger against the Americans. But there was still room for a dash of Scouse humour. One of the most photographed banners read: 'One DIC is better than two.'

That the two 'DICs' had fallen out added substantially to the turmoil. As Parry would later say: 'It soon became clear that they had very different philosophies on how the club should be run: one was hands off, the other hands on.' It was a shambles, and when it emerged that Parry had also met Klinsmann, it further soured an already troubled relationship with the manager.

If Hicks and Gillett were the wolves of Wall Street, Liverpool fans were self-appointed guardians of the club's 'earthly virtues'. Unlike the owners, they had got their act together and were trying to reach LFC's broader fan base. Paul Rice, ex chair of Broadgreen Labour Party said: 'After the Klinsmann story became clear I remember thinking, "Something's going to have to be done here. Someone's going to have to stand up to these."' He got a mate, Dave Elder, a New York financial expert, to explain in layman's terms how the deal had been set up. And how the battle could be fought online as well as in the papers and on news bulletins. It confirmed people's worst fears and crystallised the issues. Shankly's granddaughter Karen Gill was a supporter. And many couldn't help but compare the words of the immortal manager with those of the current owners – 'Weetabix, Snoogy Doogy, a spade in 60 days'. At least there was no danger of having such stuff inscribed on any walls.

In March 2008, Big Tom showed how far he was from reality by vetoing the sale of 98 per cent of Gillett's shares to DIC, saying the arrangement was 'unworkable'. It was a complex deal that, with the debt, would have made their projected takeover worth more than £500m but the Texan described it as 'derisory'. It would be a costly mistake.

Back on the ground, on 21 April 2008, 440 days after the takeover, Liverpool fans took matters into their own hands at Stanley Park. Tired of waiting for the mythical spade, some 40 supporters brought a few spades of their own, donned reflective gear and hard hats, and broke the ground at the site where the new stadium was planned. Although 380 days late, protest organiser James McKenna said simply: 'This was a dig at the American owners of Liverpool Football Club.'

CHAPTER 18

There was a touch of 'we shall fight them on the beaches' about how the fans were going to defend the soul of the club. And you could understand their frustration. Talk of a new stadium had been going on for a decade. Various iterations were drawn up and there was even talk of sharing with Everton! Of many instances when we wonder: 'What would Shanks have made of this?' this didn't need to be asked.

Aware he was losing the PR battle, Hicks tried to pull a PR stunt of his own. Those with a knowledge of history would have recognised it as 'doing an FDR' – it was the fireside chat routine favoured by American president Franklin D. Roosevelt at times of crisis. This was neither Pearl Harbour nor D-Day, but for Hicks it was a crisis. Having summoned a TV crew to his Dallas mansion, he sat in his armchair supping from a Liverpool coffee mug, pained expression on his face 'as fake as the flames in his gas fire', according to *Epic Swindle*. Professing his undying love for all things Liverpool, he proceeded to score one of the biggest own goals even of his self-harming reign. In fact, he should be credited with 'an assist' as well. Brian Reade called it 'the most repulsive PR stunt ever pulled by anyone connected with Liverpool FC'. Apart from the nauseating falseness of it all, the absentee owner had called for Parry's head on worldwide TV. Steven Gerrard was just one of millions to describe it as a disgrace. 'Let's just say they had some balls. I didn't think they'd drag the club to those lengths for some money. It just showed how greedy they were,' he told Reade.

Carragher agreed: 'That's when I thought it had got past a joke. To fly a TV crew over to your house, dress your kids in Liverpool tops, and start dishing the dirt on worldwide telly, I just thought, "Oh my God, what's going on?" It was unforgivable.' He added: 'It was like your mum and dad scrapping. You don't care what they're fighting about, you just want to scream at them to shut up.'

Benitez wanted to scream at them to put up some cash. He was denied funds in the January window even though Robbie Keane was sold back to Spurs after six months. 'The failure to back Rafa in the transfer market – especially not replacing Keane at the time – may have cost Liverpool the title,' said Nevin. But amid rumours that Benitez had quit, it was revealed that Parry had agreed to bow out at the end of the season. 'My position became untenable,' he said. 'The structure we had was dysfunctional and something had to give.' It was a season when Liverpool were fancied to be champions, but they came second, four points behind Manchester United.

While Parry deeply regrets the decision to sell to Hicks and Gillett, he told the *Echo*: 'To say we should have gone with DIC is complete and utter nonsense, that would have been a disaster too. DIC as a vehicle has imploded since.' Maybe SOS were right after all: 'We were equally suspicious of both,' said Nevin.

Chapter 19

*'At a football club, there's a holy
trinity – the players, the manager
and the supporters. Directors don't
come into it. They are only there
to sign the cheques.'*

Bill Shankly

SUCH WAS the great man's impact that the date he
set foot in Anfield is still commemorated – even by a
Spaniard who knew little about him until he walked on
the hallowed ground himself. Rafa Benitez gave this
tribute on the 50th anniversary of Shanks's appointment
as Liverpool manager: 'Everything has changed in
football and everything is different in society nowadays.
Everyone has iPods or Wi-Fis and is in a hurry to
do things. But still we try to have the same ideas as
Shankly. When people talk about the "Liverpool Way",
it was always to win. We try to do this and that is our
priority if possible. We try to do things properly, like
Shankly did.' He was speaking in December 2009.

Around the same time came this improper response from Tom Hicks Junior, a board member, to a fan: 'Blow me, fuckface. Go to hell, I'm sick of you.' It's the only thing we remember him doing – but it marked a new low for an abhorrent regime. The fans, of course, were a part of Shankly's holy trinity along with the players and the manager. 'Directors don't come inti it. They are only there to sign the cheques,' he said. Now, it seemed, they were only there to insult fans.

It happened when Liverpool fan Stephen Horner forwarded a copy of an *Echo* article to the owner's son in January 2010 and asked for a comment. He got one word: 'Idiot.' After further exchanges between the pair – and escalating bile from the director – the story gathered legs and led to Hicks Jnr's removal from the board. Bearing in mind how Shankly had treated fans, inviting them into his home and making many feel as if they had been blessed, the crassness of a lowlife, who was several stratospheres above his station as a Liverpool director, was shocking. Coming on top of his father's PR stunt, the sense the club was a victim of a corporate raid gone wrong was mounting. Wolves of Wall Street? The club had fallen prey to hyenas. For Tom Hicks Senior, the negative headlines were piling up as high as the debts. The protest banners at Anfield said it all: 'Built by Shanks, broke by Yanks.'

Owed £350m, the Royal Bank of Scotland (RBS) wanted their money back. Hicks and Gillett were desperate to sell. RBS reluctantly agreed to extend their loan by six months as long as they appointed an independent chairman to find a buyer. Fearing a stitch-up by the bank – he had already been forced to replace Parry with Christian Purslow, a pal of RBS boss Stephen Hester – Hicks was wary. But they settled on an outsider, British Airways chairman, Martin Broughton. A Chelsea season ticket holder and fully paid-up toff, Broughton didn't tick many boxes for despondent Liverpool fans. They missed out on Champions League football but worse was to come. Underappreciated and undermined by the sale of some of his best players, Benitez finally gave up the ghost.

After a brief honeymoon, Purslow had slotted into Parry's role – as the manager's new nemesis. Cambridge and Harvard educated, Purslow was a Liverpool season ticket holder and even spoke Spanish. But despite a fair bit going for him, he blew it when he told a member of staff: 'This is a world you don't understand. This is business and in business I am Fernando Torres.' As an honorary Scouser, Benitez's heart sank just as it had when the real Torres needed a knee operation and would never be a Ferrari again. Also capped at the knees, Rafa would never be the real Rafa again.

His resignation wasn't as shocking or dramatic as Shanks's or Dalglish's – it had been coming – but there were still plenty of tears. It was 3 June 2010 and a mutual decision. Just to show the calibre of the man, once he got his pay-off he donated £96,000 to the Hillsborough Family Support Group. Señor Rafael Benitez Maude, to give him his full title, wasn't on the Shankly-Paisley pantheon and lost some support in that final tortured season. But, overall, he was a very good Liverpool manager who was loved by many and would be missed more than anyone thought.

A week later he took the Inter Milan job while Liverpool were drawing up a head-hunting list to be decided by a panel. Which probably explains why they ended up with Roy Hodgson instead of Dalglish. Underwhelming doesn't do it – it was Hodgson's sheer unsuitability that made him a staggering choice. He just never got the memo about what Shankly had done for the club. Experienced? Mainly in the backwaters of Scandinavia and Switzerland and around a bend on the Thames. Charisma? The M25, southern section. He was too self-effacing by half and nice to the point of deference to Fergie. Some of his signings – Paul Konchesky, Christian Poulsen and Milan Jovanovic – gave non-entities a bad name. Even Joe Cole was over the hill. They were simply not Liverpool players. If fans thought slipping from second to seventh was bad (as they had in Rafa's last season), they now had to don oxygen masks and assume the brace position.

Dalglish had been overlooked because of his time out of the game, said the board, whereas Hodgson was seen as a safe pair of hands. The problem wasn't his hands: it was his foot that he kept putting in his mouth. Fans were soon calling for his head, but the Americans were still the main target. Not content to wave banners and shout insults, a new generation of tech-savvy supporters was waging a full-scale cyber campaign. As soon as they got wind of any corporate cavalry that might save the owners, they sprang into action. They bombarded RBS and other leading financial institutions. They presented evidence of the owners' duplicity and tried to persuade any potential saviour to think again. It was at this point that Hicks uttered another immortal line: 'It's a noise we are dealing with.'

It was a different type of noise to that which had 'frightened the ball', but it was no less effective. It had to be. In the early weeks of the 2009/10 season, gates had dwindled and Anfield wasn't what it was. Off the field things were even worse. The club had still not been sold and the October deadline was in their faces. Administration loomed as a no longer unthinkable possibility. It would mean an automatic docking of nine points. If that happened, Liverpool would be eight points adrift of the bottom two. Champions League qualification? Relegation was far more likely. What would Shanks have made of it? It was nigh on 50 years since he had brought them back to the top flight and in charge of the team was a man so far out of his depth he was beyond the reach of Ocean Rescue. In charge of the club were men he would have wanted his gangster heroes to deal with. If ever there was a time for a speck of ash to get in someone's eye, this was it.

Hong Kong badminton player-turned-businessman, Kenneth Huang, made a bid and was thought to have the Chinese government behind him. It spawned the irresistible headline 'You'll Never Wok Alone'. No one was complaining about human rights now. At this point, a consortium of Pol Pot, Ivan the Terrible and the

Yorkshire Ripper might have been preferable to Hicks and Gillett. But 'the Chinese takeaway' wasn't picked up and the owners became desperate. They sought help from their cronies but by now 'the noise' was deafening. When it looked as if US equity firm Blackstone/GSO Capital Partners might come to the Americans' rescue, 14,000 emails landed in their inbox. Hicks called the senders 'cyber terrorists' but Kop Faithful, as they called themselves, got a sympathetic call from Blackstone's CEO. A front-page story in the *Wall Street Journal* followed.

Whether these hard-nosed, high-flying hedge fund merchants were really deterred by the Scouse resistance movement is open to debate in some quarters. But not in others. When Nevin was asked how much SOS had contributed to getting rid of the Yanks, he wrote: 'Almost all of it. We mobilised a lot of the hearts and minds – all that stuff done by SOS.' Asked how much of a people's victory he thought it was, he said: 'Hugely so in football, which is dominated by business over sport.' In *Epic Swindle* Brian Reade writes: 'No group of sports fans has ever left so many rich men feeling so powerless, confused and unsure about their decisions as Liverpool's did during those 44 months.' Shanks would have led the cheers.

Broughton had been busy too. The former British Airways boss showed that he was more than a match for the club's fly-by-night owners. He had insisted Hicks and Gillett give the undertaking to RBS that only he, as chairman, had the right to appoint and remove directors, and that the owners couldn't obstruct a 'reasonable' sale. And in New England Sports Ventures (NESV) and Singapore businessman Peter Lim, he had two credible bidders making reasonable offers – in the region of £300m.

This was nowhere near enough for Hicks and Gillett, who immediately tried to change the make-up of the board before the bids could be considered. Besides the two Americans and Broughton, the board was now made up of Purslow and commercial manager Ian Ayre, and it was the two new directors that the owners attempted to remove. They tried to replace them with Hicks's youngest son Mack and his assistant, Lori Kay McCutcheon, an executive in Hicks Holdings.

Recalling the story in the *Echo*, Broughton says: 'It was dropped on me about three minutes before the meeting. We started the meeting and they said the board was invalid because two of the board had been removed by them.' He took a one-hour adjournment to check his legal advice – and crucial trump card – that only he had the right to change the formation of the board.

He then reconvened the meeting to consider who would be the new owners of Liverpool FC. 'They [Hicks and Gillett] refused to take part, saying the meeting was "*ultra vires*" [acting outside its authority]. We continued with the board meeting and concluded that both bids were acceptable and we would set up a sub-committee to assess the two options. We stayed up into the early hours of the morning negotiating between the two and finally confirming that it was going to be

Fenway/NESV. It was a close decision for all of us – it wasn't unanimous – it was the position of the board.'

On the fateful day, 15 October 2010, Broughton bluntly told the court that as Hicks and Gillett had breached their promises to build a new stadium and not load debt on Liverpool, they had 'no credibility'. He added: 'I was not prepared to be their patsy.' As the most cynical Scouser had to admit, this was no 'Chelsea rent boy' – he was playing hard ball. And it didn't take long for Mr Justice Floyd to agree with him. As Broughton recalled: 'His lordship said he could find "no basis" for what Hicks and Gillett had done being justified. The true position is that in order to ensure additional loans, they had released absolute control of the sale that they are now seeking to regain.' SOS couldn't have put it better. The humiliation of the Americans was total. They were also left with a legal bill of £500,000, no right of appeal and heard that Broughton had the right to continue the sale that would leave them facing a sizable loss on their Liverpool misadventure.

'Justice has been done,' said a triumphant Broughton on the steps of the High Court in The Strand. He underlined how damaging the Americans' leveraged (debt-based) buyout had been with £185m borrowed from RBS – repayable in only 12 months – then loaded on the club to service. 'The vital thing is that all the offers have wiped out all the acquisition debt,' he said. 'That puts the club on a sound financial footing.'

There were wild celebrations in London and on Merseyside. The end for the hated duo could hardly have been worse. They were called 'untrustworthy' by a High Court judge, lost a bundle and saw their 'franchise' handed over to another group of American venture capitalists. That irony resonated more with them than the fans, whose joy at simply removing what had become a particularly malignant cancer was unconfined. Quibbles about the new guys could wait for another day.

NESV thanked SOS for their efforts. Shanks would have approved of SOS's battle too, as it was all about ordinary people – the fans – making a difference. From spades in the ground to messages in the in box, banners to barnstorming rallies, it was a people's victory. For 30 months their campaign had made it nigh on impossible for Hicks and Gillett to refinance the debt or even show their ugly faces at Anfield.

Predictably outraged, Hicks claimed that the sale to NESV amounted to an 'epic swindle' (giving Reade the title for his book) but in January 2013 legal proceedings between the club and its former owners had been concluded. They lost and walked away empty-handed. The memories they left would be of protesting supporters, unfulfilled promises and ugly battles. Liverpool FC has been in existence for 128 years, but this was its darkest hour.

Broughton declined to stay on as chairman but is still in touch with the owners and says: 'I'm very happy we found the right people; I think they're terrific owners, I really do. They delivered on Anfield, which I think is fantastic ... they brought in a fabulous manager. I think they've done everything you could ask of them really.'

Gareth Roberts sounded a note of caution when he said in 2016: 'Now we'll forever be cynical after what happened no matter what FSG say; and we're wary they might sting us in the same way. Back then we were dealing in sunshine and rainbows as we took them for their word.'

The reign of Hicks and Gillett had provided a blueprint of what not to do to a football club, and in the end the opposition was a noise that they couldn't deal with. Asked who the fans hated more, Nevin said: 'We hated both of them. Probably Gillett more so because he was such a snide. Hicks at least had an oafish, comedy appeal.'

Chapter 20

'If we could acquire this for the debt, I really feel like we would be stealing this franchise.'

John Henry in an email to
fellow investors in 2010

THE ADMISSION of 'theft' didn't come out until years later and Liverpool fans frantically googling their new owners at the time would have been none the wiser. In the troubled autumn of 2010, the most eye-catching headline was *The Guardian*'s 'Soya bean trader who changed a team of has-beens'. If they had come across Billy Beane as well, they might have got more of a sniff. Beane was the chief apostle of Moneyball in baseball whom Henry offered US$12.5m a year to manage the Boston Red Sox. At least they would have known that the new guys were willing to stump up for someone they really wanted.

What Kopites wanted most was an antipodal contrast to the two cowboys; what they got was a man of antipodal contrasts. Farm boy/city slicker, shy asthmatic/ sports fanatic, college dropout/maths genius, bookish looks/band leader, meticulous hedge fund manipulator/ risk taker. Make what you will of all that, Dr Jekyll.

Henry had kept mostly in the shadows during the final twitching of the Hicks-Gillett corpse. Broughton thought NESV had conducted themselves impeccably throughout but, to once-bitten-twice-shy Reds, Henry and his mates were tarred by a similar brush. The bristles may have been softer, but they were still businessmen, had little knowledge of the club and were American.

Broughton understood the fans' wariness but felt that NESV's record would be the reassurance they were seeking. 'I can understand why there might be an instant reaction about their being American,' he said. 'But being American is not a problem, leveraged ownership of the football club is the problem. If you look at the Boston Red Sox, they've taken a major traditional team, previously successful but not at their peak, and resuscitated it to be a winner.'

True, but still there were doubts and a slow start did little to dispel them. The talk was of frying pans and fires, and Nevin invoked the old 'meet the new boss, same as the old boss' line. But there were parallels between the Boston situation they inherited and this one – and there they had played a long game. After due deliberation, they had kept the Red Sox at their famous old stadium. Here, NESV chairman Thomas Werner said: 'We recognise that Liverpool Football Club is an historic institution ultimately grounded in the community and the fans. Our first step as new owners will be to listen. We want to hear from the manager and the players and those who are part of the daily operation of the club.'

Between their predecessors and the new guys, fans could already discern a difference. With NESV there was no bombast – only a willingness to start consultations. Paul Tomkins's *Tomkins Times* is a byword for balance and incisive analysis on all things Liverpool, which is why Henry took him to lunch. Asked for his take on the owners, eight years on, this is an abridged version of what Tomkins wrote in his blog:

'When Liverpool was close to administration in 2010, someone had to buy the club. FSG (then NESV) did so, when fan initiatives couldn't raise the money, and while FSG haven't pumped billions of their own money into the club, they have operated it on strict, sensible principles – selling players when a ton of money is offered and putting that money back into the transfer kitty (and learning not to rush to spend it on the wrong players); revamping Anfield, with an increased capacity, and now with a state-of-the-art new training complex in Kirkby; improving marketing and merchandise; and keeping the wage-bill within the generally accepted sensible parameters.

'Debt isn't being heaped on the club in the way it was under the previous owners. FSG also realised the quality of a manager like Klopp, and paid him and his staff big money, because they knew he could get more value for money in the transfer market given how he improved players. FSG's reputation in America was always much better [than their predecessors], from what I could tell. They had brought success to the Red Sox, whereas Gillett and Hicks mostly left chaos wherever they went.'

Taking over a club in a relegation battle might have seen heads roll in some places but not with these owners. One of the first things they did, though, showed how they revered baseball's Mr Beane and raised expectations they were about to apply a version of Moneyball. Besides being the brains behind the theory and 'star' of the movie (played by Brad Pitt), Billy Beane was a massive football fan and recommended the well-connected Frenchman, Damien Comolli, to be director of football. Like Beane, Comolli had made his name spotting young and unheralded players.

To those in Boston, this move was typical of the owners' sometimes left-field thinking. Rather than sack a manager who had fast become a joke, they gave him a chance and tried to fix the team in a different way – the transfer window was coming up and Comolli would be expected to produce some rabbits. But both scribes and supporters could have told them that Hodgson was the biggest casting catastrophe since George Lazenby played James Bond. At his presentation, with a picture of Shankly on the wall behind, Hodgson insisted the coaches who had influenced him the most were Don Howe and Dave Sexton. Witnesses swear that Shanks's expression changed. On the field, with Torres now wearing his wantaway look, there was no passion, no drive. The team was un-Liverpool but as Nevin wrote in the *Anfield Wrap*: 'Hodgson just couldn't help being Hodgson.'

Self-deprecation is a quintessentially English trait, but unfortunately for him Liverpool is England's least English city. And not even an old Corinthian would have called Northampton Town at Anfield a 'formidable challenge'. But Hodgson did and he was right – they were formidable enough to beat Liverpool on penalties in the League Cup. Compare that to Shanks's systematic dismembering of opponents as illustrious as Manchester United. They said Hodgson could 'self-efface for England', which he would do – to no great effect.

The idea of a 'safe pair of hands' couldn't have contrasted more starkly with Shanks's unbridled ambition. The Scot's constant boosting of Liverpool morale and refusal to accept defeat even when the result was in the paper ... It was ridiculous at times but instilled a spirit in the club that was almost religious in nature.

Deep down, Shanks may not have believed it either, but he used it as a weapon and with it became a master of psychological warfare. Under him everything about Liverpool was the best in the world from the players to the fans to the pitch and the newly flushing toilets. And he repeated it as if it were a mantra – which he acknowledged in the 'Chairman Mao' speech. 'I've drummed it into my players, time and time again ...' he said. He was a tautologist to Hodgson's apologist. It was a wonder the Englishman didn't insert 'only' in the 'This is Anfield' sign.

Fans voted with their feet and by January contempt for Hodgson was palpable. Two days after losing to Blackburn, the owners put him out of his misery. Although his place in history looks assured – the club's worst-ever manager – it required an SOS to a cruise liner in the Persian Gulf to get his successor. By this stage, the Kop would have stumped up for a SWAT team to bring in Kenny Dalglish. 'The King', who hadn't hidden his feelings about being overlooked, was on holiday with his wife, Marina, but he duly answered the call.

Although he lost the first two games (one in the FA Cup to United) he had them in the top half by the end of January. The ship had steadied, and the clamour was for him to get the job permanently. The month ended as dramatically as it had begun with Comolli involved in a transfer window-closing frenzy during which Torres was sold to Chelsea for £50m with two strikers coming in: little-known Uruguayan Luis Suarez from Ajax for £22.8m and Newcastle's Andy Carroll for £35m. Little did we know then how ludicrous those prices would come to look.

Liverpool ended the season sixth – not high enough for European football but a lot higher than had once been feared. Dalglish was duly given a three-year contract and he and Comolli got to work on strengthening the side. There was an inevitable clear-out, but the recruits were modest in fee, although few were Moneyball material. Stewart Downing (£18.5m) and Jordan Henderson (£16m) were the most expensive, with Charlie Adam for £6.75m and Craig Bellamy on a free.

In truth, it was neither one thing nor the other. In Dalglish's first full season, Liverpool laboured to eighth in the league and relative success in the cups was scant consolation. They needed penalties (against Championship side Cardiff) to win the League Cup but lost to Chelsea in the final of the FA Cup. The electric Suarez was the only bright spot.

In March, the owners changed their name to Fenway Sports Group (FSG) – critics claimed it was the only decision they had made. The biggest one was still to be taken – about the stadium. They were perceived to be dithering but, as they had in Boston, they were going about their research with a CSI thoroughness. But what Henry hadn't considered when he was wooing fellow investors were Anfield's surroundings.

Aware that expansion of the ground would be necessary if a new one wasn't built, the club had been buying up houses for years. These Victorian terraces might once have made a set for *Peaky Blinders* but were being 'tinned up' with sheets of corrugated iron covering the broken windows and kicked-in doors. Even then, druggies and rough sleepers would find a way in. Most decent people had moved out and the area went into a downward spiral. John Henry is a stats man, but he wouldn't have liked these. Those who remained were among the poorest one per cent in the country. Life expectancy was six and a half years shorter than the average, 43 per cent of kids lived in poverty.

What had made matters even worse was the demolition of the one local beacon of activity for youngsters. The Vernon Sangster Sports Centre, or 'the Verny' as it was affectionately known, had been bulldozed to make way for Hicks and Gillett's new stadium in Stanley Park. No spade in the ground but a community hub knocked down! All this had caused the club to become hated by the very people who should have been their biggest fans. Preceding generations were. For the best part of two decades, Liverpool had taken their eye off their own backyard; Shanks would never have allowed it to happen.

Overseas visitors talk of making 'the pilgrimage' to Anfield but if any had gone off-piste to speak to the neighbours back then, their faith in the club might have been shaken. It was a microcosm of modern Britain: foodbanks cheek by jowl with corporate excess. As stark as a third-world country, where life literally changes across a railway line. Here it was clinking glasses in sponsors' boxes to doling out beyond-expiry-date foodstuffs. And millions spent on players. It's a wonder the locals didn't put up an alternative sign that read: 'This is also Anfield'.

Chapter 21

'Liverpool were a mystery to me.
I knew virtually nothing about
English football.'

John Henry

HENRY'S BRUTAL honesty made a change from the 'I've supported them since I was a boy' line often spouted by new owners. But it was hardly reassuring. It came out, quite matter-of-factly, in a *Guardian* interview a year after the takeover. Like the scoop on the Hicks and Gillett debt, its impact was limited by the paper's low circulation. But it still stoked a smouldering concern among sceptics. And Tom Werner hardly rode to his partner's rescue when he blurted out: 'I had been in sports, so I was aware of the EPL [English Premier League] and its strength globally. But I didn't know the inner workings of it. I certainly knew about Manchester United.'

Oh dear. There are Pacific atolls and sub-Saharan hamlets acutely aware that Liverpool and Manchester United are each other's kryptonite; but not in parts of that parallel sporting universe across the pond, apparently. It gets worse. At some billionaires' inner-circle meeting before buying the club, Werner recalls: 'I wasn't paying too much attention. Frankly, I was on my BlackBerry, dealing with more pressing issues. I thought there was no way John was going to drag us into that one.'

Little did he know it, but in the eyes of Kopites, their future chairman was committing seven deadly sins in two sentences. 'That one.' The empire Shanks had built, and Paisley had built on, Yeats and St John, Hunt and Callaghan, Keegan and Toshack, Dalglish and Rush, Gerrard and Carragher, Anfield, all the trophies, all the fans, the Kop, the global diaspora, European royalty … reduced to 'that one'. It was up there with Weetabix and Snoogy Doogy, so you can see why there were doubters. And the inner circle was in another solar system to the Boot Room. Financially, culturally, socially, sportingly, you-name-itly. As far removed as brainstorming sessions can get. Another rotation in the proverbial grave, another gust off the Mersey, please – someone else needed to get something in their eye.

But to be fair, Henry and co. tried hard to make up. To educate themselves about their new asset, they treated leading lights among supporters' clubs and journalists as personal tutors. And unlike with the Dow Jones, they were taking no risks. They had – eventually – put the team in the safe hands of a club legend, while with the pressing issue of the stadium, they took their time.

Henry's instinct was to remain at Anfield. Having asked Ian Ayre, the first time he saw it, 'Why would Liverpool ever want to build a new stadium?', it was clear he liked it. And having renovated Fenway Park in Boston, he had form for staying. It was always going to be the cheaper option but that wasn't the only consideration – Anfield was worth a goal a game in mythology and not far off that in reality. There was just that niggly problem of a tiny bit of the third world living next door.

When it came to personnel, though, FSG didn't mess around. In April, Comolli was sacked after being unable to find the bargains expected. He has since claimed that Henderson was the final straw. Lifting Old Big Ears came seven years too late. Overall, the team performances hadn't been good enough – and not even Suarez could make up for a third successive failure to qualify for the Champions League. He couldn't save Dalglish either, the Scot's services being dispensed with a month later. It felt harsh, but Dalglish had been a stopgap in the first place and was not of the generation they had wanted. And he hadn't been helped by his star player.

When United's Patrice Evra accused the Uruguayan of racism in October 2011, the saga just ran and ran. Suarez's claim that the offending word 'negrito' was inoffensive wasn't bought by an independent commission. He was slapped with an eight-match ban plus a £40,000 fine. His team-mates and manager backed him with supportive T-shirts but to many – especially black footballers and sponsors Standard Chartered – the gesture felt tacky and misjudged. For 'the King' to wear one was deemed less than regal behaviour. The owners stayed silent until Suarez refused to shake hands with Evra before the return match. The issue made news in the United States and sparked FSG into action. But their eventual criticism of 'El Pistolero' seemed belated at best.

It didn't stop them from offering him a new contract at the start of the 2012/13 season. Nearly two years into their tenure, FSG were finally making a few decisions, but they still called for patience. Said Henry: 'It will not be easy, it will not be perfect, but there is a clear vision at work.' On the second anniversary of their takeover in October, he announced the club would be staying at Anfield. 'There is no doubt Anfield is the spiritual home of the club,' he said. 'The Kop is unrivalled, and it would be hard to replicate that feeling anywhere else.'

By now a new team boss was in place – and he definitely wasn't like the old boss. Brendan Rodgers, 39, was one of the new, blue-sky thinkers among managers and had pipped Roberto Martinez in a two-horse race. After Hodgson and Dalglish, FSG were set on a younger man and, with most of Europe's heavyweights not available, there were only two serious contenders. Neither had managed at this level before and were simply banking on having over-achieved in the Championship with Swansea and Wigan, respectively. There wasn't much to choose between them. In the end, Rodgers's gift of the gab and 180-page dossier won by a short, perma-tanned head from the Spaniard's bubbling enthusiasm.

But he needed to convince Liverpool fans, with many finding him a bit too glib for their liking. Some had to be reminded that Shanks himself had arrived from the old Second Division. Rodgers had a so-so first season, using the chequebook modestly with modest results – seventh place was only one better than the previous season and he didn't get past the fourth round in either cup. Unusually, his two winter recruits would turn out better than his three summer signings. In January, for a combined £20.5m he brought in Daniel Sturridge and Philippe Coutinho. But once again the campaign was dominated by Suarez. The Uruguayan scored 23 goals in the Premier League and 30 in all to end up second to Gareth Bale as the players' player of the year. No less than 64 per cent of Liverpool fans had him as the club's top man.

He might have been a messiah, but he couldn't stop being a naughty boy. In April 2013 at Chelsea, he took a bite out of Branislav Ivanovic's arm – the second such offence of his career – and was hit by a ten-game ban by an independent panel. Unplayable but uncontrollable, he was what you might call a loose cannibal.

You cannot help but wonder how Shanks would have handled him. He would have loved him as a player – never-say-die, able to wriggle through a nest of vipers and still find the top corner. And for all his peccadilloes he was a team player. But Shanks had never had to deal with anybody quite like the Uruguayan. In his day,

Yeats and St John hopping on a bus instead of running back to Anfield was the most serious transgression. It would surely have been a love-hate relationship – and the ultimate test of his man-management skills.

Although Rodgers made Suarez train on his own, Henry, now able to recognise a world-class player when he saw one, was determined to keep him. Suarez's exit clause was a relatively low £40m, and when Arsenal boss Wenger cheekily tried to pry him away with an offer £40m plus one pound, all it triggered was an unusually humorous response from Henry: 'Just what are they smoking over there at the Emirates?' he asked.

What he did sanction, though, was the fly-on-the-wall documentary *Being Liverpool*. It split opinion and revealed Rodgers's portrait of himself along with his infamous envelopes. For many it was too close and personal for comfort. No one thought Shanks would have given it houseroom.

Rodgers spent more in the summer of 2013 and the arrivals of Simon Mignolet and Mamadou Sakho were attempts to address defensive concerns. Everyone knew that this season the Ulsterman had to win something – or die trying. But Liverpool had to begin it without their talisman – six of the ten games Suarez had to sit out were in the new season.

The Reds still made a good start, but once Suarez returned, they went to the top of the league. He and Sturridge were dubbed the new SAS partnership and they had the exciting young Raheem Sterling in support. They obliterated most opponents and after 11 straight wins looked set to end the title drought. Then came the infamous slip by Steven Gerrard at home to Chelsea, followed by an even more catastrophic collapse at Crystal Palace when they let a 3-0 lead become a 3-3 draw. Manchester City gleefully took advantage. Rodgers's efforts didn't go unnoticed; the owners gave him a four-year contract and the League Managers Association made him Manager of the Season. Gerrard would say his 'one-on-one management was the best I've ever known'.

But in the summer of 2014, it was clear Suarez was leaving – for Barcelona. His wife's family were there and Barça were prepared to pay the £75m that Liverpool wanted. But not before he sank his teeth into someone else. This time he was playing for Uruguay in the World Cup and Italy defender Giorgio Chiellini was his victim. He was given a nine-match suspension. It didn't deter Barça, and reaction was mixed – as much as the fans loved him as the ultimate 'man to have on your side', he was trouble. Bolstered by that record figure, Liverpool lashed out £117m on ten players in the summer transfer market. Most surprising was Mario Balotelli, a late £16m replacement from AC Milan for Suarez. First choice had been Alexis Sanchez, but he opted for Arsenal. If Suarez had 'baggage', what was Balo carrying? Nope, this wasn't Moneyball – more like money down the drain. But if the Italian was a gamble, hopes were still (relatively) high.

But not for long. Balotelli wasn't the only flop – the whole team stuttered, equalling the club's worst start in half a century. With no respite in Europe – Liverpool lost in Basel and Rodgers played the reserves against Real Madrid – they were pale shadows of the previous season. The surrender to Real probably grated most and was something you cannot imagine any of Rodgers's predecessors doing, least of all Shanks. Not only did it confirm suspicions that the manager was too clever for his own good, it turned out to be the first draft of his suicide note. It was one of many lows of a desperately disappointing season. They stumbled to sixth in the league and bowed out in the semi-finals of both cups. It was a sad way for Gerrard to sign off. Sterling also departed to Manchester City amid much acrimony. Rodgers wouldn't be too far behind.

With the once-feared strike force of Suarez, Sturridge and Sterling now reduced to an almost permanently lame Sturridge, Rodgers made attack his priority in the transfer window. But once again his recruits were a mixed bag – Christian Benteke (£32.5m) and Lazar Markovic (£19.8m) the major disasters. Even the successes – James Milner for free, Joe Gomez (£6m), Roberto Firmino (£29m) and Nathaniel Clyne (£12.5m) couldn't prevent another sluggish start.

The 2015/16 season became make or break for Rodgers. He was now three years into his stint with £300m spent and had nothing to show for it but an epic near-miss. But what persuaded FSG to act then was the availability of a certain Jürgen Klopp. Having taken a break after his wondrous years at Dortmund, the German was the man FSG had wanted all along.

Unable to prise him away when he was at the height of his success and popularity with the Yellow Wall, Liverpool's owners were minded to try again. And after a run of one win in nine games, the board wielded the axe. Rodgers was sacked one hour after a 1-1 draw with Everton, but the decision had been taken the day before. It felt a tad harsh to some but inevitable to others; Rodgers was always going to be more David Brent than Bill Shankly.

It was another decision that divided the Liverpool faithful. In his role as a pundit for Sky TV, Jamie Carragher was damning about the owners: 'At this moment their track record in making decisions for Liverpool Football Club over the past two or three years has not been good enough. It's miles off.' Whatever the opinion of Rodgers, FSG knew they had to get the next one right.

Chapter 22

*'He's the white Barack Obama ...
both are bearers of hope, both are
idols. At Dortmund, they're so fired
up that him cleaning his glasses in a
semi-competent manner brings out
cheers on the south stand.'*

Ex-Germany midfielder
Mario Basler on Jürgen Klopp

FIFTY-FOUR YEARS separate their births, and in football such a gulf might be measured in astronomical units. More than 1,000 kilometres lie between where they grew up – one in the heart of Europe, the other on the north-west fringe. One acquired a sports science degree at university, the other learned – quite literally – at the coal face.

When first asked to be a manager, the college boy compared it to 'a kamikaze mission'; the pit boy said it was his 'destiny'. Yet despite these obvious and huge disparities, you don't need forensics to find similarities between the man the Germans call Kloppo and the one and only Shanks.

Both hail from off-beat parts of their respective countries, had strict, fitness-fanatic fathers, and elder sisters who mothered them. Both played lots of football as kids. But where Shanks might have been born to be a manager, Klopp had management thrust upon him. He was nowhere near as good as Shanks as a player, never threatening to make it into *Die Mannschaft*, whereas Shanks was a fully fledged Scotland international.

Klopp was still very much an integral part of the Mainz 05 defence when handed the reins as a coach in 2001. Regarded as 'the real captain' by his team-mates even though he didn't have the armband, he steered the apparently doomed club to safety. He was appointed coach on a formal basis for the following season. Mainz were a small club, although not as small as the bleak outposts where Shanks had cut his managerial teeth. Like the Scot, Klopp was popular with team-mates as well as fans, his personality playing as big a part in his rise as his coaching skills. Whereas Shanks had left school at 14 and embraced the time-honoured Scottish way of 'pass and move', Klopp had graduated from Goethe University in Frankfurt. You have to wonder how useful this was for someone who came up with *gegenpressing* – he did his thesis on walking.

It's widely believed that the seeds of the pressing game were sown in Klopp's mind by his mentor at Mainz, Wolfgang Frank. They used to talk for hours about tactics and Klopp will say that Frank had a great influence on him. But could it be that the idea came to him from watching kids? As a student with a young wife and baby son to support, he was given DM400, a winter jacket and a season ticket to look after Eintracht Under 10s! 'I wasn't sure I wanted to do something like coaching but I needed the money,' he told Jonathan Northcroft. 'And I loved it.' He was playing Third Division football at the time too, but youngsters of that age are never shy about chasing the ball. And Klopp admits: 'I didn't have a philosophy at that stage – I was a kid myself. I was 21.'

Blessed with the rare combination of height – he's 6ft 3in – and pace – he played up front and even on the wing, and was signed by Eintracht but never made it out of the reserves. He later joked: 'I had Fourth Division talent and a First Division head. That resulted in the Second Division.' Mainz came for him in 1990 and, after scoring four times in a 5-0 away win, he harboured hopes of making it to the top flight. But no move quite happened, and he ended up with the second-tier club for whom a relegation battle was almost an annual season-long fixture. Recognising a deep thinker when they saw one, Mainz tried to use his 'head' by sticking him in midfield before eventually settling on him being a defender. He modelled himself on Stuttgart centre-back Karl-Heinz Förster, saying: 'I have always been interested in attitude more than talent – and his mentality was exceptional.'

Klopp ended up at right-back, which many say is the easiest position on the field. So, what was a tall, thoughtful and pacey player doing there? Well, it at least afforded him an excellent vantage point to study the game. We can see from his 11-year spell, in a variety of positions, how different aspects of coaching were coming together. And all the time he was benefitting from the wisdom of the obsessive Frank. He may not have realised it, but he was more than ready when the call came.

After that initial Houdini act, he followed it by finishing fourth two years in a row. And then, in 2003/04, he finally led his Mainz team into the Bundesliga top flight. It was the first time in their history, but not the proverbial 'promised land' – no one thought they would ever do it. But, on the smallest budget and in the smallest stadium in the league, Klopp pulled it off. He even got them qualification for the UEFA Cup before getting relegated the following season. He stayed one more year before Borussia Dortmund (BVB) came calling.

Leading Mainz into the big league was like taking Workington or Carlisle to the old First Division, but even those Shankly-managed clubs weren't as hand-to-mouth as Mainz. The club may have had electricity, but at one stage it had just one employee – a part-timer who sorted the mail. The announcer moonlighted as ticket seller and at Christmas collected funds to buy tracksuits. Klopp and Shanks could have swapped stories about coming up the hard way. Another common trait was how much they wanted to win – even practice matches. Just as Shanks had with his famous five-a-sides, Klopp's matches only ended when his side was ahead.

Where Klopp had the advantage over Shanks was academically. Where the Scot relied on his older brothers for tuition, Klopp believes his studies were invaluable. He said: 'Without knowing it at the time, I was working on the thing I do best and wanted to do most: coaching.' He learned about training theory, including the connection between the mental and physical sides. He goes as far as to say: 'Studying possibly saved me from an early [coaching] failure.' That's probably a bit of un-Shankly self-deprecation, as Mainz president Harald Strutz declared: 'He was predestined to become a manager.'

No surprise then that Klopp seemed to fit the blue-collar Black and Yellows like a glove. Although he was from the Black Forest, he was right at home in Germany's industrial heartland – straight-talking, no airs and graces, there was nothing Fancy Dan about him. When he was presented as the new boss, he said of the fabled Yellow Wall: 'It appeals to the football passion that burns inside me. Whoever has been down on the pitch here knows the Yellow Wall is something extra-special, one of the most impressive things you can find in football.' The parallel with Shanks's early courting of the Kop is all too obvious.

Still, BVB had their doubts. They were desperate to get this appointment right, having done 'a Leeds' in trying to live the dream – and were still suffering nightmares. They had floated on the stock exchange in 2000 – the only German club to do so – and almost sank. On the brink of bankruptcy, they endured the ignominy of being bailed out by their 'Hollywood' nemesis, Bayern Munich. It was no wonder, then, that there was a little apprehension about the next managerial appointment. Worried that he might be asking Klopp to run before he could walk, Dortmund CEO Hans-Joachim Watzke checked with former Mainz boss, Christian Heidel: 'How good is he?' Heidel told him: 'You'll never regret the day you sign Jürgen Klopp.'

Quicker out of the blocks in Signal Iduna Park than Shankly had been at Anfield, he won silverware – the German Super Cup – in his first season. Beating Bayern to a trophy and earning a solid sixth-place finish, he soon won the fans over. It would get better. The following season, operating on a low budget and using mainly young players and cast-offs, he took BVB to fifth place and UEFA Cup qualification. He said: 'It's always about making the crowd happy, it's about producing games with a recognisable style.' The BVB reporter from *Süddeutsche Zeitung* wrote: 'If Klopp trains the team as well as he does punch lines, Dortmund will soon be ready for the Champions League. It's only taken him 45 minutes to sweep BVB supporters off their feet with his infectious sparkle and eloquence. If ever a coach's mentality fit right into the football-mad Ruhr area, then Klopp's does.'

Without inviting them in for tea or crowd-surfing before kick-off, Klopp was bonding big-time with the BVB fans. And without paying big bucks he welded a team of different ages and nationalities – Poles, Croats and Japanese as well as German – into Bundesliga champions two years in a row. Most notable steals were Sven Bender for €1.5m and Mats Hummels for €4.2m, in the first leg of his career-long shuttle to and from Bayern. Bender couldn't believe how persistent Klopp was in persuading him to join, adding: 'He was a superb motivator. As a young player, he really hit the spot for me.' He did with the fans too. Once after a defeat to rivals Schalke 04, a gang of around 100 *ultras* invaded the training ground demanding to know what had happened. By admitting that BVB 'played crap today', he won them over. It might have been an action replay of one of Shanks's fan encounters.

With high-pressing and vibrant attacking, he became a raging success on the Ruhr. He had the same symbiotic relationship with the Yellow Wall as Shanks had with the Kop. The BVB *ultras* loved it when he said he was the 12th or 13th man and used the 'we' word. He really was one of them, a regular guy with no side to him, and was taking on and beating the fat cats of Europe mainly with youngsters and on a low budget. Players talked of him being 'a great entertainer' and having 'a huge presence and aura'. Fans asked if he had local ancestors – just as Liverpudlians felt Shanks might have Scouse DNA inside that Scottish exterior. Mario Basler, the former Bayern and Germany international and then a *Bild* pundit wrote: 'He's the white Barack Obama … both are bearers of hope, both are idols. At Dortmund, they're so fired up that him cleaning his glasses in a semi-competent manner brings out cheers on the south stand.'

Klopp had to warn that he wasn't a messiah just as Shanks had to deal with the quasi-religious fervour at times. It wasn't all about charisma – performance played a huge part, of course. In 2010/11 BVB were the youngest side ever to win the Bundesliga. They retained the title with the highest points in history. In 2012/13 they concentrated on the Champions League and despite being drawn in a group of death (with Real Madrid, Manchester City and Ajax) they didn't lose a game. The high point of the campaign was the 4-1 thrashing of Mourinho's Real in the home leg of the semi-final. It set up an all-German final at Wembley. But despite heroically taking the game to the big-money favourites, Bayern, they couldn't quite make it, going down 2-1. It hardly needed saying that most neutrals were on their side.

A stone in the shoe on the way to Wembley had been Mario Götze agreeing to join Bayern. Klopp said he was Pep Guardiola's favourite, but this 'exception' would become the rule – none other than Robert Lewandowski followed and then Hummels. It felt like one step forward and two back and sowed seeds not of doubt but of futility. In 2014/15, they made a poor start and Klopp said he would quit at the end of the season: 'I chose this time to announce it because in the last few years some player decisions were made late and there was no time to react. It's not that I'm tired, I've not had contact with another club but don't plan to take a sabbatical.'

He was clearly a manager of significance and had come to the attention of other top European clubs, among them Manchester United. In 2014, with the ill-fated David Moyes's reign stuttering to its inevitable end, United's executive vice-chairman Ed Woodward flew to Germany to make Klopp the offer he couldn't refuse. Deal-making was what Woodward did par excellence. He didn't just flog fridges to Eskimos, he could make the Inuit people 'United's refrigeration partners in the Arctic'. But he wasn't a football man. Klopp was prepared to listen to him and would later say of England: 'It's the only country really where I think I could work after Germany because it's the only country where I know the language a little bit.' He was willing, he was able, and he would soon be available. It was an open goal. But Woodward scuffed it past the post.

United's head honcho did Liverpool the biggest favour the club have done for them since Matt Busby advised Shanks against resigning more than five decades earlier. Klopp heard him out. The money was tempting but there was something in the job description that set off alarm bells. In trying to impress Klopp with United's omnipotence, Woodward over-egged it. He told him: 'The Theatre of Dreams is like an adult version of Disneyland.' It backfired. 'I found it a bit unsexy,' said Klopp, although he didn't entirely rule it out. Whatever you think of Manchester United, it shouldn't require too much of a sales pitch – and Woodward was a super salesman. United sells itself but if he had to push it, a football man would have sold it on Law, Best and Charlton not Mickey Mouse. Klopp decided to stay at

BVB. Liverpool didn't know it at the time, but they owe Woodward a big thank you.

In the early part of the following season when Brendan Rodgers's tenure was going the way Moyes's had at United, Liverpool's owners switched on their radar. They wanted someone who had had success at the highest level. And the Americans showed they were faster learners than Woodward. FSG president Mike Gordon said: 'I think his credentials as one of the best managers, if not the best, were apparent for all. And we like the type of football he played. Both the energy and the emphasis on attacking; high electricity, high wattage football with an appeal. So, from a football sense it was a relatively easy and straightforward decision.'

They met in New York at the offices of law firm Shearman & Sterling on Lexington Avenue. Klopp was with his agent Michael Kosicke, and right away the Americans were bowled over by the giant German – he had a personality to match his frame. Gordon could immediately see his 'enormity of substance' in which he spoke of 'activating the Anfield crowd'. The Kop couldn't hear it but that would be music to their ears as well as FSG's. After lengthy talks to find out whether Liverpool were right for Klopp as well as Klopp being right for Liverpool, they shook hands. The manager went for a walk around Central Park, leaving Kosicke to dot the i's and cross the t's. Liverpool had made their most important signing since they took a young Scottish manager out of Huddersfield.

Chapter 23

'I am the Normal One.'

Jürgen Klopp during his presentation at Anfield

FSG'S THREE head honchos – John Henry, Tom Werner and Mike Gordon – called the talks 'lengthy and substantive'. Spread over two days, the Americans learned enough – on top of the due diligence Gordon had done in Germany – to offer the 48-year-old a three-year contract. But, like their predecessors with Shankly five and a half decades earlier, did the owners *really* know what they were getting?

If they had asked the BVB *ultras*, Mario Basler or Hans-Joachim Watzke, they would have had a fair idea. When interviewing Klopp for the BVB manager's job, Watzke said: 'When he talked about "we" he had us from that moment on. No coach had ever done that.' Raphael Honigstein dubbed him a 'tracksuit missionary' in his acclaimed book, *Bring on the Noise*. When they used a giant picture of him to boost season ticket sales, the posters said: 'Vote Klopp'. Fans did and BVB had to halt the stampede at just under 50,000. They could have asked anybody; he was so popular in Germany everyone said he could be president if he stood for it.

Liverpool fans had long given up dreaming that they could ever find a manager who could be described as 'the new Shankly'. After all, even Paisley wasn't – although a 'new Paisley' would have had them dancing in the streets. A 'new Fagan' too. Dalglish *had* returned but failed to live up to his first coming. Long before then the mould had been well and truly broken. And for all the excitement aroused by Klopp's arrival on 8 October 2015 – 30,000 people tracked his flight from Germany – no one dared dream that a new 'messiah' had landed in their midst. But given his reputation as a people's man and the real similarities between Dortmund and Liverpool as clubs, this tall, smiling, casually dressed 48-year-old from the Black Forest got their attention.

His presentation was the most impressive anyone had seen, let alone from someone speaking English as a second language. He said: 'It is not a normal club – it is a special club. I had two very special clubs with Mainz and Dortmund. It is the perfect next step for me to be here and try and help.' There was no wild boast, he simply stated his intention to deliver trophies 'within four years'. It was measured but he gave a taste of his wit when he said: 'I am the Normal One.' It was brilliant even if it may have been thought up beforehand. He hit just the right notes, found just the right tone – dare it be said, he looked the perfect fit.

But he didn't have a magic wand. His first game away at Spurs was a dull, goalless draw. Two more draws followed. The players had put themselves about a bit more and he gave them bear hugs when they came off, but that was about all outsiders could discern. Too early to tell. His first win came against Bournemouth, which saw Liverpool through to the last eight of the League Cup. Then came an impressive win at Chelsea. But a shock home defeat to Crystal Palace ensured that no one got carried away. So poor was the performance that many fans left Anfield early and Klopp said he felt 'pretty alone' out there. But just over a month later a much-improved effort in a draw with West Brom had Klopp lining up his players in front of the Kop. Ridiculed in some quarters, it was actually a clever piece of crowd engagement of which Shanks would surely have approved. No one left early after that – well, not for a while anyway.

If this was to be a period of consolidation – and Klopp let the transfer window pass without a significant signing – it wasn't without excitement. With the squad now showing more spirit and energy – the term *gegenpressing* entered the Premier League lexicon – Liverpool progressed to the final of two cup competitions. But it was also not without controversy.

The first major faux pas by FSG came in February when the club announced new pricing for the following season. It would include seats in some areas of Anfield costing £77. It was an unthinkable price and the unthinkable happened – at least 10,000 Liverpool fans walked out while a match was in progress – in the 77th minute. The Reds had been leading Sunderland 2-0 but promptly conceded two goals and had to settle for a 2-2 draw. Coincidence or karma? There were other protests too, and marches – organised by SOS. They did the trick. Immediately, the club performed a U-turn and announced prices would be frozen at current levels for the next two seasons. In an apology to fans, Henry, Werner and Gordon said: 'The three of us have been particularly troubled by the perception that we don't care about our supporters, that we are greedy, and that we are attempting to extract personal profits at the club's expense. Quite the opposite is true.'

The owners were shaken – Americans pay highly for their sport and FSG, who didn't think they were doing anything untoward, were taken aback by this reaction. Still, it was a massive climbdown. The timing wasn't helped by only having spent £5.1m (on an unknown Serbian youngster, Marko Grujic) in the transfer window just gone. At least the giant new stand was taking shape even if the team still had a way to go.

After losing to Manchester City on penalties in the League Cup Final, Liverpool seemed determined to make up for the disappointment. Beating United in the Europa League brought that tournament to life and then they edged Klopp's old club BVB, of all teams, in a thriller at Anfield. Villarrreal were safely negotiated in the semi but a second-half collapse against Seville meant they had lost both finals. In the league, it was an eighth-place finish and no European qualification.

It wasn't quite the script expected but the owners had seen enough. In July they signed Klopp and his staff up to six-year contract extensions.

His summer transfer dealings suggested he was sticking largely to his Dortmund template of improving players and picking up bargains. Only two newcomers, Sadio Mané (£30m) and Georginio Wijnaldum (£25m), cost more than peanuts. Joël Matip came for free while Loris Karius and Ragnar Klavan cost less than £9m combined. But there was a clear-out with 16 players shown the door, Christian Benteke the priciest at £27m. Altogether they raised £76m while spending just £62m. That might have brought happiness to the accountants but the fans didn't expect a title challenge – top four being the limit with a squad still lacking top quality in key areas such as defence, goalkeeper and striker.

A topsy-turvy August confirmed those doubts, but September saw the opening of the magnificent new stand christened with a 4-1 win over champions, Leicester City. A crowd of 54,000 was Anfield's biggest since 1977 and here, at least, was tangible progress under FSG. The redevelopment of the fabled arena showed the owners used their hearts as well as their heads – the stand has not only increased capacity, the tinned-up terraced houses were gone and the spacious surrounds and the Hillsborough Memorial have transformed the area. An even greater leap forward was clinched on the final day of the season when Liverpool secured fourth place and were back in the Champions League – at least in the qualifiers.

The summer of 2017 was when the transfer market lost touch with reality. The Premier League as a whole spent £1.4bn, while Paris Saint-Germain enticed Neymar from Barcelona for a world-record £198m. But Liverpool were still conspicuously shrewd. They paid Roma £37m for Mo Salah – by some distance, he would be the signing of the season. Alex Oxlade-Chamberlain, who had never broken through at Arsenal, raised a few eyebrows at £2m less, but the hope was that Klopp would unlock his unfulfilled talent. Ditto Andy Robertson, who cost a paltry £10m from relegated Hull City.

But the signing they really wanted, they mucked up. Virgil van Dijk had been a tower of strength at the heart of Southampton's defence and had expressed his interest in following a well-beaten path from St Mary's to Merseyside. It was perhaps the cosy notion that Saints were Liverpool's feeder club – five players having already joined from there – but the Reds had to apologise for tapping him up – and ended their interest. Apparently. But when the window reopened in January, Van Dijk got his wish and Liverpool got the man their fans had been crying out for. But it cost them a world-record £75m for a defender. If this wasn't a statement of intent, then what was? At a stroke, Liverpool solved their back-four problem and FSG ended all doubts about their commitment.

But the buying didn't finish there. The Reds had been pursuing Leipzig midfielder Naby Keita for months – and getting nowhere. But they finally struck a deal – for £48m, although he didn't arrive until the following season. Not only were FSG backing their manager, they were prepared to wait for the man he really wanted. And Klopp was showing the kind of persistence Shanks had in his pursuit of Yeats and St John.

Recruitment had been reformed since the confusion of the Rodgers era. Now there was a director of football, Michael Edwards, who has proved a great judge of a player and interpreter of stats along with data guru, Ian Graham. And then there's Klopp, who wants to meet any prospective big signing to see what they're made of. Character counts as much as ability for him. It has the best bits of both Moneyball and Boot Room worlds.

Overseeing it all is Gordon, FSG's go-to man, whom Klopp calls 'my person'. Another key cog in the hierarchy is CEO Peter Moore, a native Scouser who returned from a corporate career in California. Moore, Gordon, Edwards and Klopp – plus academy head Alex Inglethorpe – are a transatlantic team but have a unity of purpose not seen since the Shankly era. Edwards also sells well – Philippe Coutinho finally being allowed to go to Barcelona for £142m. A constant presence at Klopp's side on matchdays was his Bosnian Serb assistant, Zeljko Buvac, whom the German referred to both as 'my brain' and 'my right hand'. The pair had been together since their Mainz days.

After basically forfeiting the League Cup and FA Cup (resting key men in both), in early 2018 Klopp was reminded of what Shanks had said: 'Liverpool exist to win trophies.' More than two years into his reign and still without any silverware, his response was: 'I am sure he didn't say it after one day or one year. The team he had and the fantastic success was when you had a team that stayed together and got better together. There were seasons when you only needed 12 players in your squad. That's a good situation, a fantastic manager, outstanding club, football-crazy city – just go. We cannot compare those times with these times.'

He added: 'If you could bring Bill Shankly back into the club now and ask him "are you happy with fourth?" because he was a fantastic football manager he would have seen that this is the only way we can go. You need to do what we are doing to be in a position to win something one day. To just want it more desperately than other clubs doesn't make it more likely to happen. That's how it is. You need to do all your homework and when the time comes, you have to catch it. Bill would have seen that 100 per cent – but unfortunately I never got to know him as a person and that's really a shame because we are doing the same job.'

By now, others were making comparisons with the great man. James Lawton said: 'Klopp evokes the spirit of Shankly, bringing the half-forgotten past back to life.' He also quoted Ian St John, who had been grudging in his praise of previous foreign managers. 'At Dortmund he inspired both the players and the people brilliantly and the same thing is happening at Anfield,' said St John. 'These are early days, of course, and no doubt there is fine-tuning to be done, but, however you look at Klopp and his work, you see the kind of passion – and knowledge of players – which were the very foundations of Liverpool's success. It is great to see them back in place.'

But Liverpool were doing well. The 2017/18 season will be remembered for Mo Salah's passable impression of Midas: everything the Egyptian touched turned to gold. No one thought he would be this good and he spearheaded Liverpool's attack, which now consisted of just the Fab Three – and no one was missing Coutinho. But there were other massive improvements. The arrival of Van Dijk made a huge difference, as did the emergence of Robertson at left-back, while Oxlade-Chamberlain was showing what Wenger had missed – especially in a thrilling win over Man City. But still City were too far gone in the league – it was the Champions League where they could be beaten, and they were.

A 3-0 win at a raucous Anfield ensured survival in the return but peak was reached in the semi against Roma when Liverpool stormed into a 5-0 lead in the home leg. But the Ox's serious injury and two late goals made for a few nervy moments in the return before they got through. Also troubling was the abrupt exit of Buvac, leaving Klopp conspicuously alone as he prowled the technical area. At first, Liverpool maintained it was for 'personal reasons' and only 'temporary', but there were rumours of a row. A split in the hierarchy was the last thing needed as the biggest game for a decade loomed. But Klopp – at least outwardly – didn't seem affected by it and was a reassuring voice when the club released a marketing campaign called 'This Means More'.

The short film opens with views of the stadium and the manager saying: 'This is Anfield, these are our streets, these are our routines, this is our home.' The Shankly statue is shown, with Klopp stating: 'This is the man who started it all.' After special mentions for the Kop and Kenny Dalglish, it doesn't brush over the bad times. But most touching is the finale: 'For others it's sport, for us it's a way of life. They have a stadium; we have a home. They have songs; we have an anthem. They have a manager; we have a guardian. They have supporters; we are a family. We are Liverpool.'

It was hard for fans not to be moved when they heard it, but, inevitably, there were critics – from other clubs. It had more than a touch of Arsène Wenger's old phrase, 'Everyone thinks he has the *prettiest wife* at home,' but what resonated most of all was Klopp's voice – not only did it suggest that Morgan Freeman had a rival, it highlighted what a perfect fit he is at this club.

And so to the Champions League Final. Critics pointed out that the German had lost his last five finals – three with Borussia Dortmund and two, the previous season, with Liverpool. He was also without Buvac. But the way Liverpool took the game to Madrid, there was nothing wrong with the preparation or the tactics. For 20 minutes the Reds dominated – then fate declared it wasn't to be. The slings and arrows of football fortune have never been more outrageous – the mugging of Mo Salah, the Loris Karius calamity and the Gareth Bale wonder goal might have been scripted by Shakespeare and Liverpool were the victims of all. But there was no Red fan who wasn't proud of the performance, and less than 48 hours after the final, Brazil's Fabinho joined from Monaco. Nothing like a big signing to take minds off a defeat – even one as cruel as this.

Suffice to say that another world-record fee (at the time) was shelled out on a goalkeeper – Brazil No.1 Alisson Becker from Roma and then Xherdan Shaqiri arrived for a bargain £13.75m from Stoke. Wow! No campaign was needed to tell fans 'FSG means business', and 2018/19 looked like being *the* season.

Buvac didn't come back and Dutchman Pepijn Lijnders, who was more popular with the players, rose from the youth ranks to take his place. But with Fabinho and Keita slow to make an impact, the Ox out long term and even Salah not looking the same, in the early weeks the Reds weren't at their refulgent best. But they were solid at the back, were winning matches they let slip a year ago and Fabinho gradually proved his worth. They went head-to-head with City in the league but, in the Champions League, left it till the last match before sealing qualification from the group phase. Then came the storybook stuff. A brilliant performance at Bayern ensured passage into the semi-final but a 3-0 loss in Barcelona – that could have been 4-0 – was simply the springboard for one of Anfield's greatest – maybe the greatest – nights.

Surpassing the Miracle of Istanbul in goals scored, Liverpool overturned the deficit before a disbelieving Kop. Old-timers recalled Inter Milan, Saint-Etienne,

Chelsea and Olympiakos but many felt this beat them all. This was Barcelona and Messi. This wasn't possible. But urged – beseeched – by an electrified crowd, Liverpool produced a comeback that was beyond anything that either Shankly or Paisley had ever seen.

It paved the way to a sixth 'European Cup' victory, over Spurs, who had produced a similarly storybook comeback to beat Ajax in the other semi-final the night after Liverpool's semi. The final was an anti-climax, but it was one of those where only the result mattered and they got it. Six times the name is now inscribed on the old trophy and only Real and AC Milan have kept the engraver busier. At home, City refused to be caught and Liverpool had to settle for second, just a single point behind. But in Europe fans claimed they were 'royalty'. A socialist club? Shanks would have known what they meant.

Chapter 24

'He's the nearest thing I've ever known to Shankly. He's got the same leadership qualities, his natural enthusiasm. Look at the T-shirt Mo Salah wore. "Never Give Up", it said. That's the mentality Klopp's brought. And it is very Shankly.'

Peter Hooton on Jürgen Klopp

IF HE'S no longer 'getting in the eye' of opponents, he's still very much in the hearts of Liverpool fans. Right and left ventricles. And although Shanks will be remembered long after the Liver Birds have flown away, the Klopp comparisons have probably helped towards the resurgence in interest almost four decades after he died.

Peter Hooton's comments came after the win over Barcelona. After the triumph in Madrid, an elderly fan called Klopp 'Shankly No.2' on Sky News.

Even Shanks's grandson, Chris Carline, can see the similarities. Hooton is a leading authority on the great man, having written the acclaimed *The Boot Room Boys* and taken part in the pilgrimage to Glenbuck that was featured in *Shankly: Nature's Fire*. Lead singer for The Farm and SOS committee member, he says of Shanks: 'He was Liverpool's spiritual leader and he had this connection with the Kop that was like a communion. And he talked in those terms – he said, "People don't go to church, they come to Anfield." He was more than a manager.'

For Klopp to even be mentioned in the same stratosphere as Shanks shows there's more to him than bear hugs and bollockings. He too has an aura and a special relationship with the fans. And the seeds may well have been sown with that infamous salute after the West Brom game. Thirty months later, lining the whole squad up in front of the Kop to sing 'You'll Never Walk Alone' after the club's greatest comeback victory was another masterstroke of public relations – or was it just from the heart? It's the same man who joined the fans in Kiev, gutted and bleary-eyed, to sing, 'We saw the European Cup, Madrid had all the fucking luck.' You have to give such a man the benefit of any doubt and Liverpool fans have – in spades.

From the moment his wife Ulla told him back in Germany: 'If Liverpool come for you, that is for you,' to the eulogies he's now hearing, Klopp can be forgiven for believing it might be his destiny. After all, the comparisons have been coming for a while.

Mark Lawrenson made his mind up as early as 2018 after the win over Roma. The stalwart centre-back of the 80s declared: 'We talked about him [Klopp] improving the players. He gets the history of the football club; he really gets the supporters and knows generally it's a working-class football club. I'm always loath to compare people but there's definitely so much of Shankly in him, there really seriously is. He's a completely different version, but a modern-day version of Shankly ... I'm not getting carried away because they've got to the final. It's just the way that he is.'

There were quibbles that such praise was premature, but more good judges are coming round to Lawrenson's view just as they are to the idea that Shanks wouldn't have been lost in the modern game. We've seen a few already in these pages and the list is growing.

Speaking to Omnisport before the Champions League Final, Australian winger Craig Johnston said: 'I was at the club a long, long time and the name Bill Shankly would always come up. There'd be a story from the old guys like Tommy Smith. Having seen dozens of managers come through, two words come to mind ... Jürgen Klopp. You're mentioning him in the same breath as Bill Shankly. You don't have to say much more. When talking about Klopp, I think heart, love, desire, passion, knowledge, craft, team spirit, fantasy because he has a touch of the fantasist about him and so do the Scousers. He has a sense of humour. He's genuinely funny. He recognises the Scousers like Shankly did. He wasn't a Scouser.'

Redoubtable 90s centre-back Dominic Matteo can see it too. On a visit to Kuala Lumpur, the Scot told me: 'Whenever you see clips on TV, they are always showing stuff on Shanks. You're just like "wow" – it's so good you want to go out there and play. There are definite similarities between him and Klopp. I was an apprentice when Liverpool last won the league. The thing I always go back to – the way I was brought up – was about bringing the ball out from the back, keeping the ball, especially in the positions I played in. It was about looking after the ball, the Liverpool Way. It was always "build up, build up, build up" and John Barnes, playing in midfield, was still trying to make that happen. But we did go a bit more direct later.

'Klopp is very inspirational. When he speaks, you listen. You can learn from him. When he speaks, it goes quiet and Shankly was the same from what you hear. Walking into a room there's respect there. And I think Jürgen, like Shankly, tries to make it light-hearted. They both talk about the fans and the players and make you feel a million dollars.'

Stephen Lawrence, son of Tommy, recalls: 'My dad used to say what a great man Shanks was. He was not just about Liverpool FC; it was about the people of Liverpool and giving them a team they would be proud of. You can see in Klopp that he feels the same about the club when he hits the Liverpool crest after a game and walks over to the fans – which is what Shanks did – he's passionate about making the club great again. Liverpool is a completely different place now Klopp is here. Like

Shanks's teams, fans are excited about how they're going to play today; the passing and movement of players is the same now as in Shanks's time.

'But I don't think he would have approved of the wage bills now. My dad fell out with the game as he could see it wasn't about playing for clubs it was about how much money they would be getting. Shanks, I don't think, would have allowed it unless it was for the benefit of the club or the people of Liverpool and he would have told them straight. He made sure he got what he wanted. It was not about the money with Liverpool, it's about the football, and playing your best for the fans, which my dad loved.'

George Scott wrote in Red and White Kop: 'There are many aspects of the modern game that Bill Shankly wouldn't have liked or been comfortable with as the game is so vastly different from the one he knew and loved. Bill was a very strong socialist and he believed passionately in the power of the team over the individual whilst still loving the brilliance and talents of those great individuals he admired, in particular the great Tom Finney.

'However, I think he would, without doubt, have adapted to the current game, much in the same way that another avowed socialist and fellow Scot, Alex Ferguson, did throughout his managerial years at Manchester United. Unlike Ferguson, however, Shankly stayed true to his socialist ideals, never moving from the semi-detached house in the West Derby suburb of Liverpool, or drinking wine and champagne, or owning racehorses, but, unlike Ferguson, he was never awarded a knighthood.

'I am not so sure how Bill would have dealt with all the ancillary things in the modern football industry. But there is no doubt in my mind that he would still have inspired the modern player with his passion and rhetoric. And he would still have been adored by the fans. The modern media would have loved him, too. But it remains to be seen if he could have coped with the incessant exposure that the modern managers are subjected to on social media and satellite TV channels. I shudder to think how he would have dealt with modern agents, though, as he always wanted to be in total control of the signing of players.

'I think his pet hates would have been the lack of empathy that some modern players have with supporters and their obsession with money. Shankly was only motivated by winning, and he would not stand for any evidence of laziness or lack of discipline. Playing for the jersey and the support was everything to him. He possessed an undefinable God-given charisma that rubbed off on everyone who crossed his path.'

Paul Moran, son of Ronnie, who played 379 times for the Reds, was twice caretaker manager, and another Boot Room sage, believes: 'Shanks would have rated Klopp because he always seemed to appreciate people who had passion for the club and a strong belief in doing the things that helped the club achieve success. Klopp always comes across as being loyal to his players as well, which is something Bill would have appreciated. I honestly believe that the way players are today wouldn't have been a problem to Bill. He would have had rules for the players that they would have followed and, although it is a different world now, players would still have been fully aware who was in charge.'

Trevor Birch, Shanks's last signing, went on to become an accountant and make a name as football's Red Adair, putting out fires at clubs facing oblivion. He says: 'I think Shanks would have loved Klopp. He liked big people such as Ron Yeats and big bubbly characters like Kevin Keegan with great charisma. Klopp's style of play is also reminiscent. Shanks started pass and move, high tempo and that, effectively, is how they play now. So, yes I think he would have loved him!'

On Shanks's ability to adapt to today's game, Keegan has grave doubts. He told *Shankly: Nature's Fire*: 'He wouldn't like it now. Looking down, he'd have hated the corporate side, players' headphones, advertising – he liked just the badge on shirts. That was the best era. Klopp might take them back and do everything all over again, but the first time is always the best.'

Straight-talking former Liverpool trainee Tony Murphy also takes a slightly contrary view on certain aspects. He claims: 'Shanks always asked the players to respect the fans, but he too shunned them at times and, to be honest, some fans are a nuisance. The game has not changed in my opinion. The external shenanigans don't play any part – it's the media who perpetuate the myth.'

On how Shanks would have handled the different owners he says: 'I think he would have adapted as he was very open to other people's ideas – hence the Boot Room.' And foreign players? 'He had no prejudice. If a player was honest and committed it would not matter if he came from Mars. I know he hated cheats and anybody who failed to give 100 per cent and this included anybody whose focus was on anything but football. So he would almost certainly have put up with modern trends from those that complied, but woe betide anybody who didn't. I don't think footballers today are any different to those in the past. Being a footballer is one of the hardest things to do and Shanks would know this.'

If you thought a Greek exile who grew up on Merseyside but is now back in Greece might have a different perspective, think again. Nassos Siotropos is still a Reds fanatic and believes: 'Liverpool Football Club is very special to the supporters and is not only about the glory – we are a very emotional club. Apart from the triumphs, we lived the tragedies and there is a family spirit, which is all down to Shanks in my view. I believe Jürgen Klopp is a very good manager but even better as a personality. I think Shanks would have loved his passion and enthusiasm. I want to believe that some of the old aura of the club is still there at Anfield and the actions of people like the Spirit of Shankly organisation helping poor people with food banks is an example of socialist principles.'

Fans reacted to the triumph in Madrid's Metropolitano stadium with mild disappointment at the football played but were unanimous in saying that it was only about the result. The relief in the Liverpool players' faces – and those of the fans – was palpable not so much because of the heat – draining though it was – but the far greater burden that history threatened to thrust upon them. Failure would have meant they had nothing to show for one of their finest seasons. It would have been a third successive final they had lost under Klopp and sixth in a row for the manager. Labels such as 'chokers' and 'nearly men' would have littered the airwaves and headlines. Although there were mitigating circumstances in all those previous final defeats, notably in Kiev, the 'loser' tag would have been hard to shake off. And especially after coming back from the dead so spectacularly in the semi-final. And all on top of getting 97 points in the league and still not ending the title drought. The scale of the celebrations showed that this was much more than a consolation prize – even if the league was the one they really wanted.

But now it has all changed. Now the talk is of the win being the start of something special, a new dynasty under Klopp with the owners rushing to offer him a contract extension. The removal of that increasingly pesky monkey from his own back was universally welcomed and long overdue. But it wasn't without a certain poignancy: it took the manager to a level that Shankly never reached – that of a 'European Cup' winner. We've seen how cruelly the Scot was denied his chance at that and it will be some time – and several more trophies – before we can put the two on the same summit overall. But Klopp is at least well beyond the foothills.

Just as arguments rage about the respective merits of sporting giants of different eras, the circumstances and challenges these two men faced on arriving at Liverpool could hardly have contrasted more starkly. Where Shanks built the club from the foundations, Klopp took over one that needed merely renovation and had billionaire backing in place. But it was also divided after years of acrimony and had fans who were becoming disillusioned. A generation had grown up knowing only false dawns, while many drifted from the game altogether, disgusted at the direction in which it was heading.

But perhaps the toughest task Klopp faced was a balancing act that Shanks could never have imagined: to bring success while maintaining the club's ethos and traditions when all about them were losing theirs. In short, he had to compete with zillionaire and nation-state owners yet still maintain the pretence of a people's club.

The dumping of a country's – or an oligarch's – oil wealth into the transfer kitties of rivals was something the great man didn't have to compete with. And although Liverpool has wealthy owners, it isn't a benefactor club – it's self-sufficient – and as Shanks's grandson Chris Carline says, 'We have managed to do it in the old way.'

The club might have split asunder without careful handling. It has capitalist owners wanting to make a buck and mainly socialist fans wanting to win trophies.

In other words, Klopp had to reconcile the irreconcilable. Fortunate to have bosses who are clever and willing to listen – even to the fans – he managed to keep both onside. He needed all his people skills but also a public relations man's nous. Politically, he once said: 'I'm on the left, of course. More left than [the] middle. I believe in the welfare state. I'm not privately insured. I would never vote for a party because they promised to lower the top tax rate. My political understanding is this: if I am doing well, I want others to do well, too. If there's something I will never do in my life it is vote for the right.' If the job is something of a high-wire act, he's maintained his balance.

So, too, have the owners. Dom Matteo thinks they deserve some belated credit. 'I think they've done a good job. The net spend is good. They've given Klopp plenty of money and have got a good team behind them. Results have helped, of course, and made the jobs easier. But the two biggest signings were exactly what we needed – a keeper and a centre-half – since then the defence has been a strong point. What FSG have done with the infrastructure is very impressive. The fan zones they've built at the back. The facilities have improved and it's still like a people's club.'

As Klopp said when the 'This Means More' film showed the Shankly statue, 'He is the man who started it all.' Klopp is the man who is carrying it on – and has put hope back in people's hearts.

Chapter 25

Chris Carline

IT SEEMED only right to ask a member of the family what they think of how Bill Shankly would have coped with today's game as well as the comparison with Jürgen Klopp. The great man's grandson, Christopher William Shankly Carline, to give him his full name, and co-owner of the Shankly Hotel in the centre of Liverpool, kindly gave his views.

I start by suggesting there's something of a return to the Liverpool Way.

'Jürgen Klopp and my granddad have a lot of very similar traits. My granddad had this thing about fans and socialism, and Jürgen has got a lot of that about him. You can look at the quotes of my granddad over the years and it was always about the fans. Everybody together and the Holy Trinity of football being the players, the manager and the fans. I think Jürgen certainly has that in him. You only have to look at how he orchestrates the crowd at games, and when he goes out on to the pitch at the end of games and does that fist pump to the Kop ... he gets everybody going and that feeling between him and the Kop is something we haven't seen since me granddad was there – at least not to that level.

'I think a lot of his philosophies about football and life are certainly similar to my granddad's and that brings with it the inevitable comparisons. I think it's fair to say there are comparisons. Like the improvement in the team since he took over. We are now genuinely considered title challengers every year. And in two European finals in two years. So, you can see the enthusiasm on the pitch – and now we've won a major trophy. It all kind of comes to nothing if you don't get that silverware.'

Did you agree with Klopp that the win over Barça was better than a trophy?

'I can see that, and I can get on board with that, and his point is really well made. You look back to that Barça game, you look back at the atmosphere, you look back at the achievement and togetherness. And the players all lining up in front of the Kop that night to savour doing the impossible against a team of the calibre of Barcelona ... I can see his point of view. It was almost like winning something and the feeling around the ground was exactly that. I am a traditionalist, however, and if we hadn't won something then in many ways it would have counted for nothing.'

How old were you when your granddad died?

'I never actually got to meet him. The story in the family tree is that he had two daughters, Barbara and my mum Janette. Barbara had three kids – all daughters. My mum had had my two elder sisters, so by the time she got pregnant with me, my granddad had only ever had two daughters and five granddaughters. No grandsons. When my mum knew that she was pregnant, he said this is definitely a boy this time – he was sure. But, unfortunately, when she was only three or four months pregnant, he passed away unexpectedly in September 1981. I was born in March 1982.

'When I was a kid, my nan Nessie Shankly and everybody else used to say that I reminded them of Bill. "Mannerisms and even from the way you walk and the way you speak," they said. There were times when I'd get up to go and get something and she'd get quite emotional and say, "You're just like your granddad."

'One story I always tell is when I was about 14 and we'd played Leeds on Good Friday when they had Jimmy Floyd Hasselbaink and Alan Smith. We got beat, and when I was a teenager, I used to be a nightmare to be around if we'd lost. I'd been going to games since I was about seven and just didn't want to speak to anyone, I'd be agitated and pacing around. We'd gone back home after this Leeds defeat and I was pacing around everywhere, and I went into the kitchen. Something from somewhere made me do it but I picked up a towel and started cleaning the top of the cooker.

'Now if you know your stories about my granddad, you'll know that if Liverpool ever lost, he would do one of two things: he'd come home and either clean the oven or mow the lawn. I'd never seen this story, and no one had ever told it to me. And yet there's me, his grandson, in the kitchen after we'd lost to Leeds, wiping the cooker. My mum came in and suddenly stopped in her tracks and went white. Then she told me the story about my granddad cleaning the cooker. And there's me all those years later stood there cleaning the cooker after we'd lost. So, I have so many traits that he had as well.'

How do you think your granddad would have handled the owners and the big money in today's game? He believed in sharing socialism yet today you've got to have a billionaire behind you. How do you think he would have coped with that?

'I get asked that a lot and people bring up agents and the money they take from deals. The first thing is that he wouldn't have liked it. Secondly, he would have adapted because he would have had to adapt. Like it or not, it's the way the game has evolved. Sadly. You've got two choices – you can either keep up with it and take it for what it is, or you don't. And if you don't, you get left behind.

'Look at Man City and what they've achieved as a team. All the money coming in compared to when they didn't have any money. They wouldn't be doing what they're doing now. Like Chelsea. They wouldn't have done anything without being bought. I'm a bit of a romantic and find it quite sad that gone are the days when a team had a group of players they brought in when they were young, put 'em in the reserves for a few years. And then in a few years' time they would start winning trophies. I think it's sadly gone now. Look at the teams that are successful – all have fairly rich owners.

'I think my granddad would have adapted to that – he might not have liked it, but I don't think it would have changed his philosophy on life or the game. Or the way he went about things. But there'd have to be an appreciation of what happens if you suddenly inject £250m into a club.

'Liverpool have found a balance. And Jürgen Klopp has. But you've got an irony. We've got billionaire owners and can afford to go and buy Virgil van Dijk for £75m, Mo [Salah] for nearly £40m and [spend] £60m on a keeper. We have injected a substantial amount of cash to get where we are. We can't say it's all been built on style and hard work – that's not the case. We can't say we haven't gone down that route – we have – but we've got a manager who still has traditional ideals. And we've still got our identity. We're lucky we've got history. We are Liverpool FC and the majority of our success over the years has been built on the old way of doing it. Bringing in players, nurturing them, working hard, shaping a team and eventually getting our rewards for it. So, we're lucky in that we can always say over our history we did it the right way, the way it was supposed to be done.

'Chelsea are the biggest case in point of doing the opposite of that. A smallish kind of club with very little success, not great facilities, a ground that's not great. Never really won that much, just the odd trophy here and there, but then, all of a sudden, a billionaire oil magnate comes in. And they've got this whole new identity. I think it's fair to say that everything they've won they've bought and everything they stand for now came through him [Roman Abramovich]. Liverpool are different. Everything we are now is based on what we've been previously. The hard work, the Boot Room, all that side of it. We're just lucky that in addition to that we've got owners who have a relatively large amount of money as well. And that allows us to still compete at the top end of the game. It's kept us there, but no one can deny that we got there through the right means.'

What about the owners? What do you make of them?

'The owners know they've got something special. Over the last couple of years, Liverpool fans have warmed to them more. And now they've fully accepted them. There were doubts when they first came but that's normal. Liverpool fans, by our very nature, are insular and we see ourselves as kind of on our own. A bit different from anybody else. When outsiders come in at that level, we're always going to wonder "do they get what we are?" Anybody who knows anything cannot deny that Liverpool FC are special. We've achieved special things and I said the other day there's no other club on the planet that could have achieved what Liverpool achieved that night against Barcelona. I'd argue that with anybody.

'So, it's fair to say this place is special. When the owners first came in, we'd had our fingers burned by the previous American owners and there was a fear of it happening again. But what won the fans over was that they've always been very honest from day one. In complete contradiction to the previous owners. We were promised a lot of things by the previous owners – and they never made good on any of them. Whereas, I think John Henry and Fenway have been very honest. They're businessmen and they said they came here to run a business. And they never overly promised other than they were going to save the club, run it as a business and try and make it profitable.

'They chipped away at that and the fans had a bit of a "will they? won't they?" attitude. But once it became sustainable behind the scenes the investment in the squad came in. They didn't oversell and they delivered. We now have a sustainable structure at the club, and we can move forward. They haven't got in people's faces either. They haven't thrown themselves in front of the cameras or in the media. Quietly, I think, Liverpool fans have taken to them. They've stayed and given the club a platform to thrive on the pitch. They've redeveloped the stadium. That new stand is unbelievable and they're going to get the Anfield Road End redeveloped as well. They've invested in Melwood and a whole new training ground next to the academy [in Kirkby]. When you look at what they've done, you really can't take anything away from them. And as for staying at Anfield, I've always preferred to stay put.'

Asked about the quotations adorning the hotel, he reveals that two contributors to this book have been honoured – Steve Darby and George Scott.

'I know of Steve – his story's here. We asked fans to give their best story and we got 60-odd and put them in the rooms of the hotel. It says "My Shankly" and gives the story underneath. There's a different story in each room. That was the concept. George Scott's is my favourite – even in the direst of circumstances when you're being released … you can make someone feel ten feet tall.'

Only Shanks could do that. And maybe Jürgen.

Chapter 26

The Man Who Had Tea with God

by Steve Darby, Liverpool-born, widely travelled coach of several nations

I'VE OFTEN been asked why I am a Liverpool fan. It's not easy to explain to a non-football person and immediately needs no explanation to a football person. I was lucky, I was born four streets from Anfield and went to Anfield Road school. Every day I walked past the ground and always made sure I touched it.

I remember my first game. I was six. It was Liverpool vs Swansea in 1961 and I was taken by my dad into the Anfield Road End with a stool to stand on so I could see. Liverpool won 5-0 with a hat-trick by Roger Hunt. It wasn't the actual game I remembered but walking up the steps and seeing the pitch for the first time. I also remembered the smells of football! Even the smell of the match programme was unique.

My dad was a Blue and also took me to every game at Goodison in the 1962/63 season and I can still recite the team. Alex Young, 'the Golden Vision', was my favourite.

Why did I choose Liverpool over Everton? I really think it was Shankly, he was like a god and when he spoke, we all listened. No one can recite a Shankly story without using his accent. You only have to watch the *Shankly: Nature's Fire* film to show the effect he had on his people. And any YouTube search will have the hairs on the back of your neck standing up.

In Liverpool they say you can change your religion and your wife but never your team! And that is ingrained in me, though I was lucky enough to be a Red in the halcyon days of the 60s and early 70s.

Sadly, I have to admit that I have felt a disenfranchisement in recent years and feel the club no longer belongs to the people (despite Klopp's efforts) as it's now a brand and a middle-class brand at that. I am not the only one and fan groups such as SOS are openly complaining and lobbying about the cost of tickets and merchandise that are pricing the working-class fan out of the game.

I was lucky enough to meet Shankly. In the days when you could visit Melwood and watch Liverpool train I used to go to watch and learn in anticipation of a coaching career. I was early one morning in 1978 and there was Mr Shankly jogging around. I thought this was the chance of a lifetime to speak to 'God' so I asked him if it was okay to ask a few questions as I was about to embark on my first professional coaching job in Bahrain.

Of course, being the man he was, he said yes! I think I asked him one question and then sat and listened for an hour, after I had made him a cup of tea. I so wished it was the day of the smartphone and I could have recorded it and for once I wouldn't care – I would have taken a selfie!

They say don't meet your heroes as you will be let down. I wasn't, he was the wonderful man I expected, and he didn't let me down. The first thing he said was I should learn to make the tea – and then I realised it was for him. I listened for about an hour, in awe and not daring to speak. He was wonderful – everything I thought he was and wanted him to be. This story is on one of the bedroom ceilings in the Shankly Hotel. Football culture beats any development programme and I've written a few for national programmes. One Shankly is worth 100 development programmes.

Chapter 27

'I love the city, love the club ...
but don't build me a statue!'

Jürgen Klopp

IT WASN'T just a monkey off the back, it was an Eastern Lowland gorilla; it wasn't a drought broken, it was the American Dust Bowl of the 1930s; it wasn't a hex removed, it was the Relief of Mafeking. Talk to Liverpool fans about how they felt when the Reds clinched their first league title for 30 years, and you get a heartfelt amalgam of all three. Like Shanks, Scousers are not averse to a bit of top spin but if it 'means more', it hurts more, and, at times, the pain had been excruciating.

The ever-lengthening lead at the top of the table had begun to dull it but then came the pandemic and the anxiety returned. It wasn't people dying in their thousands that worried them, but whether the season would be cancelled. And when the null and voiders piped up, the conspiracy theorists wondered whether the virus had come out of China or Chorlton-cum-Hardy.

Then, as Project Restart began to take shape, there was the waiting. That, according to an old song, is the hardest part. And when a rusty Reds were held by Everton in the first game after lockdown, it meant the act of deliverance couldn't be at Anfield in the next match. With hindsight, it was surely a mixed blessing, as when they did turn it on to thrash Crystal Palace it was before a silent Kop.

Ghost games have all the atmosphere of a haunted house and are not the way to celebrate pivotal moments in football history. With a visit to Man City still to come, the fear was that the wait would drag on, delaying the inevitable but diluting the moment, not to mention delighting the haters. Besides being the party-pooper of all time, this format offers a kind of consolation *Schadenfreude* for jealous rivals.

Then, on an unlikely midsummer Thursday evening, it happened. It was Chelsea, of all teams, those plastic antipodeans to the people's club, who did it the greatest favour. They caught out Pep's men to ensure a guard of honour at the Etihad instead of an ambush. But you cannot get away from it: Liverpool fans' ultimate 'I was there moment' was in their living rooms.

Suddenly oblivious to the virus, thousands gathered outside Anfield and it was the biggest story of the day. The less-than-ideal circumstances couldn't diminish it or detract from its significance and we all saw what it meant to Klopp – tearing up mid-interview and, for once, lost for words.

Liverpool had not only closed the chapter of doubt, they now stood on the cusp of a new dominance. But it was still a stolen climax to a fantastic story. Asterisk season? It bore all the marks that punctuation has in its locker: kicking off as European champions, adding the Super Cup, the World Club Cup, romping to within two wins of the title, the threat of it being snatched away and then, finally, becoming English Premier League champions for the first time, and league champions for the 19th.

All that and no lap of honour! How Shanks would have milked it, and no doubt Klopp too. The next home match should have been an occasion to rank with the great European nights – Inter, Saint-Etienne, Olympiakos and Barcelona – but Anfield would remain a silent citadel. Nope, it didn't just rain on the parade, the parade didn't happen. Klopp said it would one day – when it's safe.

The German had things in perspective even before the denouement. 'I had to Google the word "asterisk",' he chuckled. 'I only knew it from the Asterix comics! But for me, 100 per cent this is the most difficult year and season to become champions. It is an interrupted season that has never happened before and whoever will become champions, it will be historical.' But he also admitted: 'I became worried in the moment when people started talking about voiding the season. I was like "wow". And I really felt it physically, that would have been really, really, really hard.'

CHAPTER 27

It was hard anyway but, in the great scheme of things, only a fleeting sliver of time, and as unfortunate as it was, it will not hold a candle to a season's memories seared indelibly into folklore or the records broken. Over time, its magnitude will overwhelm any sense of anticlimax and heal the wounds of past agonies.

This season's relentlessness was a throwback to the 1980s and had been unthinkable during those three decades of despair and dodgy owners, false dawns, near-misses and near-oblivion. Worst of all was the hated glams commandeering their perch and Fergie rubbing their noses in it. But midway through the season, the media were already acclaiming Liverpool's greatness. The *Daily Telegraph*'s Paul Hayward wrote: 'The team is already a masterpiece – it's several teams packed into one.' 'Immortality beckons' and 'Anfield back as an impregnable fortress' were other headlines. They may not have matched the 'Invincibles' but as far as the title was concerned, they were the 'Inevitables'. *The Guardian*'s Barney Ronay wrote that 'Liverpool has a chance to win as no one has won before', adding, 'it feels like they started their victory lap in January'.

When it began back in August 2019, the Reds weren't even favourites. For all the euphoria of the sixth capture of Old Big Ears, City were still a noise – to coin a familiar phrase – to be dealt with. They were domestic treble winners after all and had shown their mettle by withstanding Liverpool's nine-game winning onslaught to clinch the title by a single point.

City nicked the Community Shield on penalties, but it was the only defeat the Reds suffered in an otherwise encouraging August. A perfect start in the league with maximum points from four games had the bonus of Liverpool going top midway through the month when City surrendered two points at home to Spurs. If only they had done that last season!

'European royalty' status was reinforced with a Super Cup win on penalties over Chelsea while Virgil van Dijk was named UEFA's Player of the Year. The only negative was a serious-looking injury to Alisson just 39 minutes into the opening 4-1 rout of Norwich. But even that had a silver lining in enabling Adrián, a late replacement for the departed Simon Mignolet, to emerge as an unlikely instant hero.

Thanks in part to the Spaniard's agility, the absence of the FIFA Goalkeeper of the Year barely affected Liverpool, whereas Aymeric Laporte's loss two weeks later almost emasculated City. With Fernandinho having to fill in, City paid dearly for not replacing Vincent Kompany and were seldom the force of last season.

The Reds maintained their storming start in the league through September but were brought back to earth by a surprise defeat at Napoli in the Champions League group phase.

Where City would slip up again – losing at home to Wolves – Liverpool's only imperfection in the league was when they were held to a draw by old nemesis, Manchester United. By the time the clocks went back, it was already a two-horse race.

When City went to Anfield in November, Liverpool's defence was given a grilling by Pep's pass masters but held firm and the attack killed them on the counter. The Reds went 3-0 up before a City consolation – a statement victory if ever there was one and greeted as such by a deafening roar. Liverpool went eight points clear.

Winning by the odd goal, winning with a late goal and winning without playing that well ... performances were already bearing the hallmarks of champions. With three successive wins in Europe ensuring passage to the knockout phase, the only smudge on the Red horizon was a looming fixture logjam. The Club World Cup was in Qatar in mid-December and something had to give. Inevitably, it was the Carabao Cup when a youth team was fielded against Aston Villa. With Klopp and his men watching on TV in the Gulf, a 5-0 scoreline was harsh on an energetic performance by the Reds' youngsters. But when the first team clinched the global crown, the sacrifice seemed more than justified.

Long derided as Mickey Mouse in Britain, this tournament has been gathering kudos. The glams had won it and having world champions on your CV isn't to be sneezed at when you have fans in places other clubs cannot reach. Thanks to Mo Salah, the Middle East and much of the Muslim world is Liverpool red. There was also prize money of some £3.5m for just 180-plus minutes' work compared to the paltry £100,000 that Carabao were offering for a five-month slog. But what really impressed was the way the team came back to hammer Leicester 4-0 away on Boxing Day straight afterwards. If anything, the trip seemed to have rejuvenated them.

The feeling that the club could do no wrong had been reaffirmed with a surprise transfer swoop. Red Bull Salzburg's Japanese attacking midfielder Takumi Minamino joined on 1 January for just £7.25m. Little known but remembered for dazzling Anfield in a 4-3 Champions League loss to Liverpool in October, it was seen as an astute piece of business. Typical FSG, typical Michael Edwards, who had spotted the low-value release clause in his contract. Shanks would have called it larceny. The best news of all, though, was that Klopp had also signed – to stay until 2024.

Prior to the capture of the title, peak Liverpool was probably at this time, around the turn of the year: manager renewing, parading the world title, a clever new signing, hammering a supposed rival in the league, opening up a massive gap and then fielding a second-string side that beat Everton in the FA Cup. Liverpool and Liverpool Reserves, indeed! On 19 January, Anfield sang 'We're gonna win the league' during a 2-0 win over Manchester United, a scoreline that did scant justice to Liverpool's superiority. At one stage, no United player touched the ball in the home half for almost ten minutes.

The Reds were kings of all they surveyed and it appeared that only a stray meteorite could stop them. But just when it looked as if they would join Preston's and Arsenal's Invincibles, they faltered. Three defeats in a fortnight in three competitions – to Watford on 29 February, at Chelsea in the FA Cup on 3 March and to Atlético Madrid on 11 March at Anfield, the latter ending their reign as European champions – took them into the foothills of wobble territory. Then COVID-19 came along and with it the lockdown.

Liverpool unwittingly grabbed the early headlines with a massive own goal. By leaping on to the UK government's furlough scheme to save 80 per cent of staff salaries, the owners were seen as insensitive and opportunist. With Spirit of Shankly and former players especially vocal, the owners were slaughtered. It was the kind of craven manoeuvre you might have expected from their predecessors.

Stung by the shellacking, they quickly back-tracked and apologised. It completed an unwanted hat-trick of faux pas when the raging capitalist instinctively sheds his people's club clothing and reverts to type. They had done the same with the £77 ticket fiasco and attempt to trademark the name of the city. It was a shocker from a club whose British CEO Peter Moore claims, 'Even today, when we talk about business, we ask ourselves "What would Shankly do?"' They couldn't have asked on this occasion.

Once the title had been secured, there was much debate about whether Klopp would build a dynasty and dominate like Shanks and Paisley did. With a 23-point gap at the time of clinching the title, such talk was inevitable. And with the manager and most of the players signed up on long-term contracts, quality kids coming through, the club on a sound financial footing and with a new £50m training ground close to completion, Liverpool FC has seldom looked healthier.

'This is not just a one-off,' said Kenny Dalglish, the last Liverpool manager to take the English championship – in 1990 in the old First Division. 'Last year they came within a point of [winning the Premier League title]... Onwards and upwards. I think there are a lot more happy days for the club.'

Even the chance of players being cherry-picked has lessened as Liverpool is the top club in the world and Klopp's 'mentality monsters' have bought into the project. Leaving would be a downgrade even if their salary might be topped up, but as long as Klopp is there, few departures are expected. He's a hard taskmaster but not draconian, has fine-tuned the heavy metal approach and, in exchange for maximum effort and loyalty, is generous with the time they can spend with their families.

Chairman Tom Werner paid due tribute but was understandably cautious when he spoke to the media the morning after Chelsea had beaten City: 'The competition is fierce and I know our rivals are working tirelessly to upend us. But we've got such talent in place as Jürgen, as Michael [Edwards, sporting director] and the team on the pitch. One of the things that stuck with me this year was their hunger for winning. I don't think that will be diminished. They're such a good group of players.'

Other similarities with Shanks, in particular, are the attention to detail, clever recruitment and selling high.

Philippe Coutinho, who cost £8.5m and fetched £140m from Barcelona was a case in point. Not only did Klopp buy Van Dijk and Alisson with the money, he tweaked the style to make the counter-attacks more lethal after the Brazilian had left.

But can Klopp emulate Shanks, who stayed at Anfield for 15 years? To beat a team as good as Pep Guardiola's City by such a margin suggests he can build on this season, but City, whether Pep stays or not, will not go away and another benefactor club, Chelsea, have already shown that the new normal for them is the old normal, with Roman Abramovich's interest rekindled. In contrast, FSG showed their prudent side by pulling the plug on the signing of Timo Werner. The signing of Bruno Fernandes has finally given United a glimmer, so the 2020/21 season offers a mouth-watering prospect for spectators if and when they are allowed back.

But none more so than Liverpool fans, who now have one of the best teams of even their illustrious history. None have ever dominated so emphatically as the 2019/20 vintage. It's a very different world to the one that Shanks knew and to achieve what Klopp has in just four years by reverting to so much of his template, he deserves all the accolades that are coming his way. 'What would Shankly do?' asked Moore. 'Keep Klopp for life' would surely be the answer.